P9-CDS-334

ON THE CREST OF THE WAVE

BECOMING A WORLD CHRISTIAN

C. PETER WAGNER

LIBRARY
BRYAN COLLEGE
DAYTON, TN 37321

Regal
Books
A Division of GL Publications
Ventura, CA U S A

88557

Rights for publishing this book in other languages are contracted by Gospel Literature International foundation (GLINT). GLINT also provides technical help for the adaptation, translation, and publishing of Bible study resources and books in more than 100 languages worldwide. For further information, contact GLINT, Post Office Box 6688, Ventura, California 93006, U.S.A., or the publisher.

Scripture quotations in this publication, unless otherwise noted, are from the *New King James Bible,* Copyright © 1979, 1980, 1982 by Thomas Nelson, Inc., Publishers. Used by permission. Others versions quoted are: *TLB—The Living Bible,* Copyright © 1971 by Tyndale House Publishers, Wheaton, Illinois. Used by permission.
Authorized King James Version

© 1983 by C. Peter Wagner
Much of this material is based on *Stop the World, I Want to Get On* © 1974 by C. Peter Wagner
All rights reserved

Fourth Printing, 1985

Published by Regal Books
A Division of GL Publications
Ventura, California 93006
Printed in U.S.A.

Library of Congress Cataloging in Publication Data
Wagner, C Peter.
   On the crest of the wave.

   "Based on Stop the world, I want to get on"—Copyright p.
   1. Missions.   I. Title.
BV2061.W347   1983   266   83-8616
ISBN 0-8307-0895-2

CONTENTS

Letter to the Reader

Some things in life are optional and some are not.

Wearing shoes is optional. But eating is not.

Driving a car is optional. But once you choose the option, driving on the right hand side of the road (here in America) is not.

Becoming a Christian is optional. But once you decide to ask Jesus Christ to take control of your life, involvement in world missions is no longer optional.

I'm not saying that these things are impossible. You can choose to go without eating, but if you do you must take the consequences. You must be willing to exist at a low energy level, to invite infection and disease, and, if you persist, to die.

You can choose to drive on the left but you will pay fines and cause accidents.

And you can reject missions even if you're a Christian. But the consequences are clear:

1. You will find yourself sitting on the bench while you could be in there playing the game. As I hope to convince you in this book, missions are on the cutting edge of excitement in the Christian life. Being left out means a dull existence as a child of God. It is less than God's best for you.

2. You will lose authenticity as a Christian. You say that Jesus is your Lord, but yet you will be failing to obey Him at a crucial point. Another word for that is *hypocrisy*.

3. You will be poorly prepared for the judgment day when what we have done here on earth will be tested by fire and only the gold, silver, and precious stones will survive (1 Cor. 3:12-15). Whatever else this means, Jesus will not be able to say to you, "Well done, good and faithful servant" (Matt. 25:23).

Many Christians aren't involved in missions because of ignorance. Their pastors don't talk about missions. Their church has no missions program. None of their Christian friends is involved. But once they hear about missions they get excited.

Others aren't involved because of a turn-off some time in the past. They may have heard that the age of missions is now over. They may have been told that missionaries are Western imperialists bringing nothing but harm to people out there in the third world. They may have heard a missionary speaker they didn't like. As a result, their general image of missions is negative.

If you happen to be one of the uninvolved, I hope you read on. Keep an open mind and I believe you will change your opinion. Missions today are not dull. There is so much new action and excitement that many missionaries themselves have trouble keeping up. More missionaries than ever before are building furlough time around study programs so they won't be left in the dust. Pastors are expanding their church missionary programs because of the tremendous spiritual lift it brings to the whole congregation.

One of the most encouraging signs of the times is the current attitude of young people toward missions. The decade of the sixties was the doldrums, but according to David Howard who directed the Inter-Varsity Urbana missionary conventions for many years, the attitude began to change in the early seventies. Now in the eighties a new movement, matched perhaps only by the massive Student Volunteer Movement in the early part of our century, has taken root among Christian students in colleges and seminaries across the country. A growing number of God's people want to be world Christians, and opportunities for doing so are multiplying.

I hope you too want to be a world Christian.

My prayer is that this book will help you become one.

C. Peter Wagner
Fuller Seminary School of
World Mission
Pasadena, California

One

Look at What God's Doing!

We are in the springtime of Christian missions.

The last couple of decades of the twentieth century hold forth more promise for the dynamic spread of the Christian faith around the globe than any other period of time since Jesus turned the water into wine.

What a distance we have come from the sixties! That was a wintertime for missions in the United States. The Western powers were retreating from their colonial empires. The Viet Nam war had pushed American morale to an all-time low. Violent struggles for civil rights erupted. College students revolted on their campuses. Young people left their homes, hit the streets, and formed the hippie movement. America was under a dark cloud of confusion, pessimism, and despair.

Inevitably, this social mood influenced the churches.

Many denominations which were not firmly committed to biblical, evangelical theology made decisions to demote evangelism and promote social ministries. One of the outcomes was a frightening membership decline in the mainline churches which persists today. Missionary programs were curtailed, sometimes because the sources of funding were drying up. A professor of missions wrote a book entitled *Missionary, Go Home.* Christian leaders began talking about a postmissionary era. Not a few wondered out loud whether the whole missionary movement had failed.

In some circles a residue from the sixties still remains. For example, the mission agencies affiliated with the Division of Overseas Ministries of the National Council of Churches were sending out 8,279 missionaries in 1969, but only 4,817 in 1979, a drop of over 40 percent in ten years. But the general trend is the other way. The total number of North American Protestant missionaries sent overseas was 34,460 in 1969 and 53,494 in 1979, an increase of more than 50 percent over the same ten years.

Yes, the ice of the wintertime is thawing and the grass is turning green. The decade of the seventies saw some of the most significant advances in world missions yet recorded. The academic field of missiology came into its own and opened new avenues of theory and practice for Christian mission. New missionary agencies began to spring up in the third world like daffodils in May. New research and receptivity advanced Muslim work to a degree that few could have anticipated. The bamboo curtain lifted in China and revealed that some of the most vigorous church growth in history had been going on all the while. Many observers have detected a fresh outpouring of the Holy Spirit "with signs and wonders following" which may be widespread enough to signal a new age of Christian outreach.

Springtime is here, and there is considerable reason for optimism.

Looking Ahead

The momentum begun in the seventies seems to be increasing in the eighties. The number of agencies and societies committed to sending out missionaries will undoubtedly increase through to the end of the century. The *MARC Mission Handbook* lists forty-seven agencies formed between 1975 and 1979. Some new ones will be established within denominational structures, some without. Mission societies will continue to start in the U.S.A. and other Western nations, but in all probability a much greater number proportionately will be formed in the third world. The number of missionaries will increase, but qualifications may change. Missionary budgets will swell, but different priorities may exist for spending the money. Strategy will be better planned. Missionary candidates will be better trained and more efficient. Every year should see more men and women won to Christ and more new Christian churches planted than the previous year.

For the first time in human history, the *World Christian Encyclopedia* reports, the Church is ecumenical in the literal meaning of the word. There are Christians and Christian churches in every inhabited country on earth. Furthermore, these Christians are more active in outreach and evangelism than ever before. David B. Barrett, editor of the *World Christian Encyclopedia,* calculates that each Christian is evangelizing 2.4 times as many non-Christians now than in 1900.

Increasing attention will be given to the cities of the world. The move toward the cities is awesome. When I was in school I was taught that New York and London were the largest cities in the world. Now there are eleven cities larger than New York and by the year 2000 there will be twenty-three larger cities. Raymond J. Bakke, the ranking evangelical urban expert, calculates that every month the world grows by two Chicagos! By the end of the century, Mexico City will have thirty-one million inhabitants. That is more people than live in all of Canada now.

Bible translation has made tremendous progress. There is some Scripture in over 1,763 languages, covering 97 percent of the world's population. But the remaining challenge is twofold. First, the Scriptures need to be translated into the remaining 3,000 languages and dialects. The notion that the dialects will disappear with the modernization of the world is a myth. In many parts of the world minority dialects are becoming more, not less, popular.

The second aspect of the challenge is to revise current translations. Bible translation technology is so advanced that we now recognize that many translations are embarrassingly inaccurate and obsolete. To help meet this challenge, the Fuller School of World Mission has recently teamed with Wycliffe Bible Translators in the first graduate program in Bible translation leading to a Ph.D. Dan Shaw of Papua, New Guinea is directing the program.

A further development which promises to widen the horizons of missionary activity over the rest of the twentieth century is the acceleration of Muslim research and training. The leader in this area is Don M. McCurry, founder of the Samuel Zwemer Institute of Pasadena, California. Probably more research has been done to develop effective missiological approaches to Muslim evangelism in the past six years than in any other similar period of history.

Students for Missions

Student interest in missions is now at a new peak. It last crested in the early part of the century with the Student Volunteer Movement. In the 1920s the SVM recruited over 2,000 missionary candidates a year, but then fell into a rapid decline. Inter-Varsity Christian Fellowship picked up the slack and, in 1946, began holding triennial student missionary conventions. They are now known as Urbana Conventions because they are held on the campus of the University of Illinois at Urbana. Along with many other conferences, the Urbana Convention felt the impact of the anti-missionary mood of the sixties. It came to a climax in Urbana in 1969 when convention director David Howard found himself "embroiled in a prolonged and heated discussion" with new staff members who doubted whether Christian missions should be emphasized that much at all. I myself was invited to address the plenary session on the topic of evangelism. At the time I was a missionary in Bolivia and rather unaware of the student feelings of the day. I was startled by the hostile reception of my stress on soul winning. Speakers who emphasized social revolution were loudly applauded.

But no longer. Inter-Varsity mission leaders such as John Kyle and David Bryant now say that instead of spending time arguing about the validity of missions, they have more than they can do in helping motivated students get involved in missions. The vast majority of the fifteen thousand to seventeen thousand participants in each Urbana Convention go away truly turned on to reaching the world for Jesus Christ. Their Student Training in Missions program has grown over 300 percent in the last six years.

A central focal point of this new student interest in missions is at the U.S. Center for World Mission, an umbrella organization founded by Ralph D. Winter in Pasadena, California in the mid-seventies. Growing out of its ministry was the International Student Consultation on Frontier Missions held in Edinburgh, Scotland in 1980. Some of the spin-offs from that may well be the seeds of a student movement for missions as large and as influential as the Student Volunteer Movement in its heyday. The Caleb Project, for example, helps college students set goals for frontier missions and shows them how to become involved. At this writing it has groups on thirty-seven American campuses and is mushrooming. The National Student Missions Coalition under Rob Larkin sent traveling teams to visit 100 campuses last fall with the purpose of starting prayer meetings for mission frontiers. Prayer groups were started on all 100 campuses! A group of Westmont College graduates, dedicated to stimulating interest in missions, now publishes a new magazine called *The World Christian Magazine* (formerly *Today's Mission*) that is aimed at the student audience. Parallel to these efforts is a Student Mobilization office designed to promote the Frontier Fellowship in the student world. And all this under one roof!

The U.S. Center for World Mission

The U.S. Center for World Mission is itself a remarkable sign of the times. Founder Ralph Winter resigned from the faculty of the Fuller Seminary School of World Mission in 1976 and struck out by faith to purchase the former campus of Pasadena College, a Nazarene school now at Point Loma, California. The U.S. Center has become a beehive of activity for the promotion of missions. The miracle story of how this happened is told in *Once More Around Jericho,* written by Roberta Winter who along with her husband was the co-founder. The stated purpose of the center is to stimulate a movement for frontier missions throughout the United States. Frontier missions may be defined as the evangelistic activity that focuses on the 16,750 unreached groups of people in the world which do not as yet have a witnessing Christian church in their own culture. They help missions, churches, and students to become meaningfully involved. Divisions of the center include mission strategy, mission mobilization, mission training, and mission services.

In addition to the fact that personnel in the U.S. Center have backgrounds in sixty-four different mission agencies, organizations and activities directly sponsored there include: training English teachers to go to other countries and teach English; the Institute of International Studies for college and university students; the Career Foundations Program providing a year of studies between college and career involvements; the William Carey International University headed up by Virgil Olson; and others. Dozens of cooperating organizations have leased space on the campus and contribute to the center's activities. The Episcopal Church Missionary Community, the Chinese World Mission Center, the Institute of Tribal Studies under Don Richardson of *Peace Child* fame, International Missionary Advance which promotes indigenous missionary movements in third-world countries, and the Fellowship of Artists for Cultural Evangelism are just a few of them.

Perhaps the most far-reaching creation of the U.S. Center for World Mission will prove to be the Frontier Fellowship. The Frontier Fellowship aims to enlist one million Christians for daily prayer and study around the topic of frontier missions. Inspired by the report of Christians from the Lushai tribe in Burma, who set aside a handful of rice at each meal as a contribution to their mission outreach program, a group led by Ralph and Roberta Winter conceived the idea of encouraging American Christians to empty their pockets and purses of loose change at the end of each day. The change goes into a jar (the Frontier Fellowship provides a colorful label for the jar) and is directed toward mission activity.

The key tool of the Frontier Fellowship is an attractive *Daily Prayer Guide* published every month which gives

Bible readings, vignettes of missionary activity, factual information about unreached peoples, and devotional thoughts for each day of the month. It is designed so that the mission agency, church or denomination, student group, or other entity which establishes its own Frontier Fellowship chapter, personalizes its monthly prayer guide on the covers and in a center insert. Organizations such as the Evangelical Free Church, the World Evangelical Fellowship, the Africa Inland Mission, the United Presbyterian Center for Missionary Studies, and dozens more issue the monthly bulletin and distribute it to their own constituencies. The program includes five components:

1. *Reading* daily about the world's hidden peoples in the daily prayer guide
2. *Praying* daily for the gospel to become "at home" among these groups
3. *Saving* loose change daily as a reminder to pray
4. *Gathering* each month in a Frontier Fellowship group
5. *Sharing* the frontier vision regularly with others.

If the Frontier Fellowship accomplishes only a fraction of its goal of raising $100 million per year for missions, it will prove to be an unprecedented stimulus to the forward thrust of missions in the eighties and beyond.

Missiology in Academia

Despite social conditions which could have militated against them, two significant events took place in the mid-sixties which would prove to influence the course of world missions. One was the founding of the School of World Mission at Fuller Theologial Seminary in Pasadena, California in 1965. The other was the World Congress on Evangelism held in Berlin in 1966.

Donald A. McGavran, now recognized as perhaps the most influential missiologist of the twentieth century, had a new vision for missionary education which led to the founding of Fuller School of World Mission in 1965. While some European universities had chairs of missiology previous to that, missiology had not been a recognized field of academic pursuit in the United States. At that time, degrees offered in missiology, schools of mission, and full-time mission professors were hard to come by. Now Fuller offers two master's degrees and three doctorates in the field, guided by a faculty of nine full-time resident professors in the different branches of missiology. At this writing over two thousand Fuller missions alumni are serving on all continents. In 1973 the American Society of Missiology was formed and the journal *Missiology* began to be published. Programs similar to Fuller's are now springing up at Trinity Evangelical Divinity School in Deerfield, Illinois; Biola University in La Mirada, California; Dallas Seminary in Texas; Asbury Seminary in Wilmore, Kentucky; Southwestern Baptist Theological Seminary in Fort Worth, Texas; Concordia Seminary in Fort Wayne, Indiana; and Columbia Bible College in Columbia, South Carolina.

This explosion of missiological knowledge is changing the face of missionary work. It is introducing concepts with names like *contextualization, theological education by extension,* and *E-2 evangelism* which have clarified the task considerably. Missiological technology is rapidly being translated into the increased effectiveness of field workers in concrete situations. A common lament of veteran missionaries is, "If I had only known then what I know now . . . "

The Lausanne Committee for World Evangelization

The year after Donald McGavran founded his graduate school of missions, Billy Graham gathered some of his friends to convene the World Congress on Evangelism in

Berlin in 1966. While the emphasis on new mission out-reach was not especially prominent there, it was stressed eight years later in the second such effort, the International Congress on World Evangelization held in Lausanne, Switzerland in 1974. More than four thousand persons from virtually every nation of the world gathered at Lausanne to celebrate what God had been doing and to catch a new vision of the remaining task. Two of the presentations at Lausanne, which have subsequently had a considerable impact on world missions, were a plenary session address by Ralph Winter and a research document by Edward R. Dayton.

Ralph Winter, at that time still on the faculty of the Fuller School of World Mission, argued that the highest priority of the total task of world evangelization had to be cross-cultural evangelism. He showed statistically that by far the majority of the non-Christians of the world would not be able to accept Jesus Christ if someone did not leave their own culture and engage in what is classically known as "missionary work."

Edward Dayton, director of the MARC research division of World Vision International, distributed in booklet form the first report on the world's unreached peoples. This was an effort to break down into manageable units the non-Christians who needed cross-cultural evangelism. I will explain more about this later on.

One of the outcomes of the congress was the formation of a fifty-member Lausanne Committee for World Evangelization (LCWE). I had the privilege of being elected to the executive committee of the LCWE where I still serve at this writing. I was also asked to be the first chairperson of the Strategy Working Group and given the task of expanding the research on unreached peoples. One of my first moves was to form a partnership with Edward Dayton and MARC, a relationship that has continued through the years. In fact, I recently resigned from the Strategy Working Group and was replaced by Dayton himself.

Another outcome of the Lausanne congress is almost too big to describe—the worldwide reverberations of that meeting. At least thirty other congresses, conferences, and regional or world-level meetings trace a large degree of their impetus to that meeting. By the end of 1982 the remolding of the perspective of the major forces in missions was virtually a clean sweep, particularly among Protestant evangelicals. The challenge of the unreached peoples of the world and the need to get on with the task optimistically was widely accepted. For example, *Time* magazine's Christmas 1982 cover story said, "The most important change in Protestant missionary strategy in the past 10 years has been to identify and seek to contact some 16,000 tribes and social groups around the world that have been beyond the reach of Christianity."

This focus on reaching the unreached people groups (which I will explain in more detail in a later chapter) was the major theme of the third world-level meeting after Berlin and Lausanne. The Consultation on World Evangelization was convened in Pattaya, Thailand in 1980. The role of the Lausanne movement, and especially the leadership given by Leighton Ford, the chairman, and Gottfried Osei-Mensah, the executive secretary, as well as Bishop Jack Dain, John R. W. Stott, Thomas Zimmerman, Donald Hoke, Saphir Athyal, and many others has been a major factor in moving the Christian world into the springtime of missions.

Seventy-Eight Thousand Christians a Day?

It may be rather hard to believe, but at the present time, according to our best calculations, each day welcomes a net increase of at least seventy-eight thousand

Christians on this planet. How do we arrive at that figure?

First of all we take into account the world population explosion. World population back in the days of Abraham and Moses was no doubt far less than 100 million. At the time of Christ it had reached 275 million. When William Carey launched the modern missionary movement around 1800 the world population had grown to about 900 million. It then passed 1 billion in 1850, 2 billion in the 1930s, and 3 billion around 1960, 4 billion in 1975, and reached 4.7 billion in 1983.

According to statistics released by the U.S. Center for World Mission, there were 1,362 million Christians in 1983, or just about 30 percent of the world's population.

The World Christian Encyclopedia calculates that sixty-four thousand new Christians are added each day by natural increase or so-called biological growth. But over and above this, some others are added each day through conversion from the world. No one knows exactly how many of these there would be, but one educated guess says about fourteen thousand. How is that guesstimate made?

It is based on the assumption that all across the world, committed Christians—those who are true members of the Body of Christ and who are dedicated to obeying God in all things including witnessing to non-Christians—will produce an additional 2 percent increase annually as the result of evangelism alone. The U.S. Center estimates the number of true Christians at about 259 million. Adding on 2 percent would mean 5.18 million per year or fourteen thousand per day in round numbers. In graphic form it looks like this:

1. Among nominal Christians:
   biological growth   52,000 net increase
2. Among Committed Christians:
   biological growth   12,000 net increase
   conversion growth   14,000 net increase

total daily net increase   78,000 Christians

One result is that every week approximately one thousand new churches are established in Asia and Africa alone. Most of them begin as small, struggling groups of believers meeting in a home or under a tree or in a school. But each one constitutes a definite group of believers who are committed to each other to meet regularly to worship God, to help each other grow in the faith, and to reach out in love to the unchurched around them.

Even so, churches are not growing at the same rate around the world. There is little or no growth in the Mongolian Peoples Republic, in Albania, in Libya, or in Afghanistan. Growth comes hard in France and in Bangladesh and in Israel. But in numerous places in the world the gospel is spreading vigorously. And right now a few places such as Korea, Ethiopia, China, Central America, Indonesia and the Philippines are dramatic flash points of growth. For the most part, Christianity is simply growing "out of control"!

Let's look at some of this growth region by region.

Phenomenal Growth in Latin America

In many parts of Latin America the Protestant churches are growing three times the rate of the population. Back in 1900 only fifty thousand Protestants were to be found in Latin America. The number passed 1 million in the 1930s, 2 million in the 1940s, 5 million in the 1950s, 10 million in the 1960s and by 1980 the figure was over 20 million. Some predict that by the end of the century there will be 100 million Protestants in Latin America.

Many denominational groups are seeing good church growth there. But the most spectacular has been among the Pentecostal churches. Around the middle of our century Pentecostals comprised something like 25 percent of all Protestants in Latin America. Now, thirty years later, the figure is in excess of 70 percent. The largest of the Pentecostal denominations is the Assemblies of God in Brazil which claims a constituency of 6 million. Among them, full adult members number 3.8 million. I became so fascinated by the upsurge of the Pentecostal movement in Latin America that I wrote a book called *What Are We Missing?* and attempted to analyze some of the dynamics behind the growth.

Along with Brazil, Chile has seen some of the most explosive growth in Latin America. One of the reasons for this is that Christians there regularly move right into the streets to preach the gospel in plazas and on street corners. In evenings and on weekends you can't walk far around the city of Santiago without running into a group of Pentecostals playing accordions, singing at the top of their lungs, and sharing the testimony of their faith with whoever will listen. A large number of Christians trace their spiritual pilgrimage back to hearing the gospel preached out in the open air.

One of my favorite churches is the Jotabeche Methodist Pentecostal Church of Santiago, pastored by Javier Vasquez. For years I visited them in their old building on Jotabeche Street which accommodated five thousand people. But that became entirely inadequate to handle the crowds, so they built a new sanctuary to accommodate sixteen thousand around the corner on Alameda Avenue. A balcony on one side holds the two thousand-member choir and orchestra combined. On a typical Sunday evening, when the main service is held, one thousand instruments—mostly guitars, mandolins, and accordions—will be playing while all two thousand choir members are singing special numbers. While they are singing, some worshipers will begin "dancing in the Spirit" while others shout "glory to God."

But this building is also inadequate because Vasquez's

flock numbers between eighty thousand and ninety thousand members twelve years of age and over. Members are allowed to attend the mother church only once a month. The other three Sundays they are participating in the activities of one of the many smaller "classes" located in the different neighborhoods of the city. The classes are like satellite churches. Their membership runs between 800 and three thousand and each is led by one of Javier Vasquez's associate pastors. Many of the classes have their own very substantial church buildings.

But the Jotabeche sanctuary, much larger than anything in the United States, is still not the largest in Latin America. The Brazil for Christ church in Sao Paulo reportedly seats twenty-five thousand. I say reportedly because some have contested that figure, but even if it is slightly off, it is an immense place. I visited it before it was completed. At that time the congregation was still meeting in the narthex which seated five thousand. When I asked how many pews they had, the person who was showing me around said, "I don't know—we ordered a mile and a half!"

Growth is taking place not only in the cities but in the rural areas as well. Until recently the 10 million Quichua people who populate the Andes Mountains from Ecuador to Argentina were not very receptive to the gospel. Missionaries of the Gospel Missionary Union in the Chimborazo province of Ecuador, for example, could count only 300 converts over the twenty-five years from 1945 to 1970. That figures out to be one convert a month. But the harvest began to ripen. During the seventies the Quichua church grew to thirty thousand. That averages 250 converts per month. So far in the eighties the growth has accelerated to over 800 converts per month and the church members well over fifty thousand. Most are peasant farmers who walk for days over bleak mountain trails to share the love of Christ with other Quichuas.

Traditionally, the message of the gospel in Latin America has appealed to the working class. But changes have begun to take place, and many middle- and upper-class people are now opening their hearts to Jesus Christ. Some of this is happening through the Catholic charismatic movement. But evangelical Protestant churches are also beginning to take root among the more wealthy. In Bogota, Colombia the Foursquare Church is multiplying home Bible studies in twelve upper-class neighborhoods. Some of these classes regularly have up to 100 who attend.

A pace-setting center of outreach to the well-to-do is the Lima Encounter with God project coordinated by the LeTourneau Foundation and the Christian and Missionary Alliance. Two huge sanctuaries have already been built in Lima, Peru in the Lince and Pueblo Libre areas. Another is being built in Miraflores. The Lince church has two thousand members and the Pueblo Libre church is not far behind. Evangelical leaders from many other Latin American cities are studying the Lima method in an attempt to launch similar projects in their areas.

One of the global flash points of growth is Central America. In Guatemala, for example, there were one thousand Protestant believers in 1930, but 1.5 million in 1980. According to a research report by James Montgomery of Overseas Crusades, the nation is now almost 25 percent evangelical, and soon will be much more. The Assemblies of God are currently growing at 44 percent per year. For example, one of their local churches, growing 50 percent per year, increased from twenty-five hundred in 1978 to eighty-five hundred in 1981.

Church growth in Central America seems to be taking place across the board socioeconomically. In the tribal areas, for example, Southern Baptists have seen their churches among the Kekchis grow from 225 members in 1972 to over two thousand in 1980, or 1,400 percent decadal growth rate (DGR). Some of the villages are now from 35 to 50 percent Christian. On the other hand, the wealthy classes are also responding enthusiastically. Some of their churches meet in hotels. An example is the Fraternidad Church, which has grown from thirty members in 1979 to 500 three years later. The Verbo Church has grown to twelve hundred members in just over six years, largely among the middle class. Its most illustrious member is the former president of the Republic, General Efrain Rios Montt, the first committed evangelical to become a Latin American head of state.

Similar accounts could be given of Nicaragua, Honduras, and El Salvador. One of Latin America's largest churches, Centro Evangelistico, is in San Salvador. Three crowded services are held each Sunday morning to accommodate the fifteen thousand worshipers. Analysts say that the violence, the political unrest, and the guerilla activity have turned the thoughts of Central Americans toward God, and thousands have found peace through the gospel message of the evangelical churches.

Massive Influx in Africa

If churches are growing rapidly in Latin America, they are growing even more rapidly in Africa. David Barrett says, "For one hundred years now, the most massive influx into the churches in history has been taking place on the African continent." In 1900 there were less than ten million Christians in Africa. Now there are over 200 million, and the projection for the end of the century is just a tad under 400 million. This means that Christians will have grown from 9 percent of the African population to 48 percent in our century.

One of the most remarkable phenomena of church history has been taking place in Africa during the last hundred years. Called the African Independent Church Movement, it has now spread to at least one-third of the tribes in Africa. At least six thousand of these new Christian groups (some more orthodox or biblical than others) have sprung up and include over eight million persons. Some are small with only a few hundred members, and some go into millions, like the Church of Christ on Earth through Prophet Simon Kimbangu, located in Zaire. They are growing at a rate faster than most people can keep track of. A new African independent denomination forms on the average of one per day.

On a recent visit to Kenya I had the privilege of meeting one of the independent leaders personally. In Kenya, out of a total of 240 Christian denominations, 180 or 75 percent are independent churches. Archbishop Herbert Aloo is one of the top leaders of the Maria Legio Church, but not at the top. Over the church's archbishops are eight cardinals and one person called the Pope. Aloo told me how they split from the Catholic Church back in 1962 because they felt the priests were not living according to the rules of the Bible. They still consider themselves Catholic, but not Roman Catholic. "Everything we do, we do according to the Bible," he affirmed.

Aloo was converted when he was sick. He read in a local newspaper about Baba Simeon, the top leader of the movement, and sought him out. Baba Simeon prayed for him and he was healed. Aloo and the others even call Baba Simeon "Jesus" because through him they were saved not only from disease but from drunkenness, fighting, and a degraded life. (They have no apparent theological problem with an overidentification of their leader with the Messiah.) None of the clergy receives a salary; Aloo must be one of the few archbishops in the world who earns his living as a laborer at the local airport.

But somehow all this must be relevant to East Africans. The little group of ten that began in 1962 has now grown to 150 thousand!

When I attended the Lausanne congress in 1974, I mentioned in one of my workshops the urgency of planting new churches. Afterward a Nigerian came up to me and thanked me. As we talked, I discovered that in the previous five years the Lord has used him to plant no less than 258 new churches, which have a total of thirty-four thousand believers. I calculated that to average one church a week for five years! In the same category is Ezekiel Guti, a Zimbabwean who recently visited our School of World Mission. He has been vigorously planting churches for fifteen years, and now is the leader of a new denomination of eighty-five thousand members and 240 churches. Attendance in the mother church in Harare frequently runs between eight and ten thousand. Few if any parallels to these African church planters can be found in the Western world.

The most popular evangelist in Africa now is a German missionary to South Africa named Reinhard Bonnke. He has teamed up with a black South African pastor who has a special gift of healing, and they travel through the black areas with a tent. The tent they had been using until recently accommodated ten thousand but proved to be much too small. So in 1982 they took delivery from an American engineering firm of a new tent which accommodates thirty-four thousand! It is held up with twelve hydraulically operated center poles and transported from place to place in six semi-trailer trucks.

Ethiopia has been a Marxist country since 1975. The government is doing all it can to restrict the Christian movement. But it is not being successful. Despite persecution, churches are growing vigorously. The Word of Life Churches, fostered in the past by SIM International, are adding a new church almost every week. The Lutheran Mekane Yesus Church which had only thirty thousand members in 1960, grew to 100 thousand by 1978, then spurted from 100 thousand to 500 thousand in the next two years. And all this occurred in the face of severe persecution which saw the imprisonment of the church's general secretary, Gudina Tumsa.

Gathering the Harvest in Asia

Comparatively speaking, the growth of churches in Asia has been slow. But many recent events point to the probability that the proportion of Christians to the whole population will increase in Asia more than any other region of the world. Probably the first Asian nation to become predominantly Christian will be Korea (with the exception of the Philippines which is already about 85 percent nominal Catholic).

One hundred years ago there were no churches in Korea. Now in the city of Seoul alone, there are six thousand. In 1970, 10 percent of South Koreans were Christians. By 1980 there were 20 percent. Many expect 30 percent when they celebrate the Christian centennial in 1984. In the army, the chaplains are doing a remarkable job; 47 percent of the personnel is Christian. Of 200 members of Parliament, at least sixty are born-again believers. At least three mass Christian rallies on Yoido Island in Seoul have attracted more than 1 million. The largest, held in 1980, drew 2.7 million, perhaps the largest single gathering of human beings in world history. Six new churches are started in South Korea every day.

The Methodist church began in England, but now the world's largest Methodist congregation is in Korea—the Kwang Lim Methodist Church of over ten thousand pastored by Kim Sundo. The Presbyterian church began in Scotland, but now the world's largest Presbyterian con-

gregation is in Korea—the Young Nak Presbyterian
Church with over fifty thousand members pastored by
Park Chu-Choon. The Assemblies of God began in the
United States, but now the largest Assembly of God is in
Korea—the Full Gospel Central Church with over 270
thousand members pastored by Paul Yonggi Cho.

The Full Gospel Central Church is a phenomenon in
itself. The present sanctuary, where I had the privilege of
preaching a couple of years ago, seats ten thousand. But
the walls are being knocked out and the seating will be
expanded to something between twenty-five and thirty-
five thousand. When it is finished, they will still have to
hold seven services every Sunday as they do now. An aux-
iliary fifteen-story building next door will have an audito-
rium to seat three thousand on each floor and the worship
service will be transmitted there by closed-circuit televi-
sion. The church will thus be able to serve the 500 thousand membership projected by Pastor Cho for 1984.

A key secret of Full Gospel Central Church growth has
been the establishment of nineteen thousand home cell
groups, each with a trained leader who takes the responsibility of the spiritual well-being of ten to fifteen families.
Because of this approach, no one in the massive church
feels lost or uncared for. Cho has been in such demand to
share his insights into church growth with other leaders
that he established an organization called Church Growth
International with a worldwide ministry. It is likely that he
will turn out to be one of the most influential leaders in
global Christianity in the latter part of the twentieth century.

Unquestionably, the greatest surprise in world Christianity in recent years was the discovery of church growth
in China. When the missionaries were expelled in 1949-
1950 and the bamboo curtain fell, hopes were not high. At
the time there was a total of about 1 million Chinese

believers. The efforts made by the Communist government to extinguish the Church were massive. Pastors
were jailed, Bibles were confiscated and burned, church
buildings were closed, Bible schools were disbanded,
Christian literature was outlawed, both lay leaders and
clergy suffered humiliation, imprisonment, and torture,
and most outside observers thought the Gang of Four and
the Cultural Revolution would be successful in wiping out
the Church. But as the bamboo curtain began to lift in the
late seventies, and news began to filter out, it became
clear that the Holy Spirit had remained behind in China and
was doing mighty things. The first word was that the 1
million were still there. Then the estimates continually
grew to 3 or 5 million, then 8 or 10 million, and now even
conservative estimates range between 30 and 50 million.

Northeast India is a land of tribal peoples. Seventy-five
years ago it was populated by 1.5 million headhunters.
Then the missionaries arrived with the gospel and a trans-
formation has taken place. Today at least 75 percent are
Christian. Of the largest tribes, 67 percent of the Khasis
are Christian, 90 percent of the Nagas and 98 percent of
the Mizos. A number of leaders from these tribes, whose
fathers were literal headhunters, now have graduate
degrees from our School of World Mission.

There are many other focal points of growth in Asia.
One of the greatest ingatherings into the Kingdom of God
in recent years began in Indonesia in 1965. Such a large
percentage of the population is now Christian that the government reportedly has withheld the results of the latest
religious census because they might be an embarrassment
to Muslim political leaders.

In Burma, churches among minority peoples were
growing so fast that the missionaries were expelled
twenty years ago, but the churches among the tribal peoples have kept growing. In the very north of Burma, the

Kachin tribe alone now has 100 thousand Baptist believers. The largest known baptismal service in the world was held at the Kachin Baptist Centennial Convention, in 1977, when six thousand were baptized. The number baptized on the day of Pentecost was doubled!

Missionary work had been very difficult in Cambodia (Kampuchea) through the years. Then the Communist government took over and began a horrible program of genocide. Large numbers of Cambodians fled to the refugee camps across the border of Thailand. There they opened their hearts to the gospel. The Christian and Missionary Alliance reported that twenty-five thousand of them had become believers in one year. This is five times the total number of converts that the missionaries had seen in over fifty years of evangelistic work.

These stories of God's amazing work in the world in which we live could be multiplied over and over again. But it is time now to take a look at the challenge. Much has been done, but much yet needs to be done.

The Challenge of the Fourth World

When we learn that there are seventy-eight thousand new Christians every day, that a local church in Korea has almost 300 thousand members, that a new denomination is starting in Africa every day, and that God is at work as never before recorded, it would be easy to react the wrong way. It would be easy to say, "Hey, this is great! The job is getting done much faster than I thought. I'm not really needed. I'll turn my attention on something else."

Don't fall into that trap!

In order to get the blessing, we look at the wonderful way God is bringing people to Himself and building His Church. But in order to catch the challenge, we look not at the Christians but at the fourth world.

This expression "fourth world" is one of the handiest

new phrases we have. It's so new you won't even find it in the unabridged dictionary. Since I will be repeating it often in this book, let me pause here to explain it.

Words, like clothes, can wear out or go out of style so that one has to replace them with something better. We have had quite a few outdated words in missionary work, and we are trying to get rid of them. Several words that once were useful and that had positive meanings are now disreputable. Missionaries used to go to the "heathen" or to the "savages" or to the "pagans" or to the "natives" or to a "backward people." These expressions, and others like them, are now very degrading. Something new is needed.

For some years now, the term *third world* has been in use. There is still some debate as to its precise meaning, but most people who use it refer to those nations that refuse to align themselves with either the Communist bloc headed by Russia, or the capitalist bloc headed by the United States, and that have decided to be their own masters on the international scene. This world includes, therefore, most of the nations in Africa, Asia, and Latin America. Most of the third world is yellow, black, brown, and red, and most of its people live south of the thirtieth parallel north.

"Fourth world" is not meant to describe some other form of international political alliance or nonalliance, although some attempts have been made to use it to designate the poorest of the poor. My intention is to shift the focus to spiritual things. *By fourth world I mean all those people, no matter where they are found, who have yet to commit themselves to Jesus Christ as Saviour and Lord.* There are fourth-world people in Russia, there are some in Africa, there are some in Chicago, Illinois, and there are some in every other tribe, tongue, and nation.

It is much better to talk of sending missionaries to the

fourth world than to the "heathen," although in the final analysis you're saying the same thing.

So much for the definition. Now back to the challenge of the fourth world. God expects us to do our part to reach them with the gospel message and persuade them to become followers of Jesus. Of them, about 850 million are in a position to hear the gospel from already existing churches. That leaves 2.3 billion, or 73 percent of all non-Christians, who will not even hear the gospel unless someone decides to leave his or her own culture and become a missionary. No wonder Ralph Winter argues that the highest priority of all missionary work is cross-cultural evangelism. I agree.

The Blessing and the Challenge

In summary, most Christians in America today are enjoying great blessing. I cannot think of another time in history when it could have been more exciting to be a Christian than in the latter part of the twentieth century.

I am often amused by Christians who are overly nostalgic. They say, "My, the Christian church is in terrible shape. If we could only go back to the first century, we would know what God really can do through a dedicated church." I don't think we're perfect today by any means, but I disagree with that perspective. I honestly think that if Luke himself could have the choice, he would rather live today than in the first century. When we lift up our eyes to what God is doing worldwide today, that early activity around the eastern Mediterranean seems like a small pilot project compared to what is happening now.

But, as the Bible tells us, to whom much is given, of them much is also required. We must face the challenge realistically. I hope that every person who reads this book will decide to become a world Christian. There has never been a better time to do it.

An increasing number of older people are saying, "Tell me more. I want to be fully informed about Christian missions." An increasing number of young people are asking, "How can I get involved personally? How can I buy into a piece of the action?" I hope to begin to answer these questions as this book develops.

Do Something Now!

1. Get in touch with MARC at World Vision International, 919 West Huntington Drive, Monrovia, California 91016. Ask for a free sample of the MARC Newsletter and a list of the materials they have available. Become familiar with the excellent research they are doing.

2. Write the U.S. Center for World Mission, 1605 Elizabeth Street, Pasadena, California 91104. Send $1.00 and ask for a copy of their chart "Unreached Peoples of the World–1983" and for a copy of the *Daily Prayer Guide of the Frontier Fellowship.* Try to establish a Frontier Fellowship chapter in your church, in your school, or in your small group. When the chart arrives, study it carefully and discuss the meaning of it for you and your church.

3. Read one or more of these books:

In the Gap by David Bryant (Inter-Varsity Missions). This is the best all-around tool for becoming a world Christian.

The Christian World Mission by J. Herbert Kane (Baker Book House). This is a textbook which provides a serious introduction to missions from an evangelical perspective.

What Are We Missing? by C. Peter Wagner (Creation House). This is the book on the Pentecostal movement in Latin America that I mentioned previously. Many who have read it have commented that not only did it expand their vision for the world but it also increased their faith in God. I hope it does the same for you.

Two

Are the Heathen Really Lost?

In the last chapter I mentioned that the word *heathen* is suspect these days. I still use it in the title of this chapter, however, because that's the way this classic question has been framed for many, many years. To a large extent, it is the key theological question for missions. If you're not satisfied that the answer is yes, you might as well reconsider getting involved in missions.

The first step is to be sure we understand the question. The two key words are heathen and lost.

Heathen. Since this is an admittedly unfortunate word, let's update it and say that we are referring to those people in the world who have yet to accept Jesus Christ as Saviour and Lord. That helps us understand that we are talking not just about the naked cannibals out there in Mamba Bamba but also about the fourth-world people in our own neighborhoods here in the United States. The non-Christian organic chemist is as much of a "heathen" as the cannibal.

Lost. Some will wonder if it is worthwhile stopping to define the word *lost.* It shouldn't be necessary, but it is. As a matter of fact, many Christian leaders seem to get increasingly confused over its meaning as time goes on.

The opposite of lost, of course, is found or saved. Salvation is what the lost supremely need. Jesus came to "seek and to save that which was lost" (Luke 19:10). Because in recent years so many people, especially leaders in the World Council of Churches, have been asking, "What do you mean, saved?" or "What do you mean, lost?" their Commission on World Mission and Evangelism convened a major conference in Bangkok over New Year's 1972-1973 on the subject "Salvation Today." Far from clearing up the confusion, the conference only added to it.

The book that was published to prepare delegates for the conference defined *lostness* and *salvation* in every conceivable way. Frequently *lostness* meant suffering under social oppression, and *salvation* was to come through the revolution. Salvation implied freedom from torture or humanization or victory over enemies. Salvation from sin was also one of the suggestions. But one personal testimony told of a man's lostness in ideology until he was "saved by Mao."

It's regrettable that so much confusion has surrounded a concept so crucial for missions. It is hard to believe that God's revelation could be that muddy for anyone. Why do some people want to avoid the idea that what the Bible means by salvation is, in its most profound dimension, salvation from sin and its consequences?

Until recently, even some evangelical leaders have been using the term *salvation* in a sub-biblical way to mean social improvement. But a major paper on the subject, written by Ron Sider, a leader in the Evangelicals for Social Action group, was presented to the world-level Consultation on the Relationship Between Evangelism and Social Responsibility held in Grand Rapids, Michigan in 1982. In it Sider admits that there had been a tendency to broaden the word too much and that the fundamental reference of *salvation* in the Bible is to salvation from sin and reconciliation with God. He pointed out, however, and I agree, that this bona fide salvation must also be worked out in ways that influence society. More on that later.

How is this developed in the Bible?

God told Adam that the day he sinned he would die (Gen. 2:17). Adam sinned, and that day he died. The Bible explains this in its first three chapters. From Genesis 3 on, the whole human race is described as lost in sin, and the Bible develops the story of how God took the initiative to save mankind from sin and death.

Exactly in what sense did Adam die?

Adam's death was both spiritual and physical. Spiritually he was dead because he was from that moment alienated from God and out of fellowship with Him. Physically he did not become an instant corpse, but from that moment on he was mortal—doomed to die physically some day.

Losing the Garden of Eden

But Adam's sin caused a third problem that some miss. Spiritually he lost fellowship with God, physically he lost immortality, but materially he lost the Garden of Eden. Sin produced the possibility of poverty, exploitation, war, dehumanization, social injustice, slavery, pollution, and any other social problem of yesterday or today.

As you read through the Old and New Testaments, you find that God deals with all three of these problems. Each one has many complex ramifications, and international conferences of scholars frequently meet to debate them. But it does seem that the general outlines of the solution emerge clearly, even to Christians who would not classify themselves as scholars.

The material or social problem. God made human beings to live in the Garden of Eden where material and social problems were unknown. Sin got them expelled and placed in the dog-eat-dog world of blood, hate, and filth. This did not please God then, nor does it please Him now. He wishes people were back in the garden, but the cherubim with the flaming swords are there guarding the entrance (Gen. 3:24). As a matter of fact, God Himself put the cherubim there, and only He can take them away. So far, no one has returned to the Garden of Eden, mainly because everyone is a sinner and their sin will not allow it.

God is the Lord of the universe. The Bible frequently speaks of the Kingdom of God, and He is the King. He controls every aspect of the life of all people in every nation and society. If He wanted to remove the cherubim with the flaming swords and let men and women return to the Garden of Eden, He could do so instantly. But God does not do this. The curse of Adam persists and will persist until this present age ends and the Kingdom of God is instituted in its fullness.

Meanwhile, the grace of God also persists. In this present age a foretaste of the Kingdom has come. God sends rain on the just and the unjust. Human beings are not as bad as they possibly could be. God sends prophets to announce His will. Those who accept the gospel and serve Jesus as their Lord already partake of many of the blessings of the future Kingdom. But even at best, life in this world is not like it was in the Garden of Eden.

Someday this will change. Someday those who have followed God will be taken to be with Him. It won't be the Garden of Eden, but it will be the new Jerusalem. The first book of the Bible, Genesis, tells how human beings were separated from the tree of life (Gen. 3:24), and the last book, Revelation, tells how they once again are restored to the tree of life (Rev. 22:2). The rest of the Bible tells of what happens in the meantime. Much does happen, but notice that one thing that does not happen is the total solution of the social and material problems that have plagued the world since Adam and Eve were punished for sin and banished from the garden.

The final solution to our social and material problems caused by sin, is eschatological, meaning at the end of human history as we know it. Meanwhile, God by His grace allows and encourages partial solutions to the problems and He urges us to do the best we can in living the most human life possible. This aspect of our Christian responsibility has been called by a noted theologian of mission, Arthur F. Glasser, the "cultural mandate."

If you reread the Old Testament prophets you will see how, on page after page, they thunder forth with the cultural mandate, admonishing God's people to love their neighbor more, to put an end to oppression of other human beings, to share the wealth, to live honest lives, or in a word, to be more human. Jesus declared Himself in the same tradition when He said that the Spirit had anointed Him to preach deliverance to the captives, and recovering of sight to the blind, to set at liberty them that are bruised, to preach the acceptable year of the Lord (Luke 4:18-19).

There is a real sense, then, in which God desires that the human lot be improved. But the cherubim are still there. The flaming swords remind us that we cannot return to the Garden of Eden, much as we wish we could. As long as human history lasts, quarreling, exploitation, sexual immorality, injustice, poverty, and prejudice will be a part of human life. They should remind us of the terrible consequences of sin and turn our eyes in hope toward the New Jerusalem, where the tree of life will finally heal the nations (Rev. 22:2).

The physical problem. Physical death began the moment Adam sinned, and spread to all people (Rom. 5:12). Physical death does not mean that you no longer exist after death (as in the case of animals), but it involves the separation of the body from the spirit. This is painful enough for the person whose body gets sick, is burned, suffers an accident, or whatever else might be involved in the dying process. It is even more painful for surviving loved ones who were emotionally attached to the one taken from them.

Physical sickness and death are ugly consequences of sin. A few, however, will escape death. In the Bible we have cases such as Enoch (Gen. 5:25) and Elijah (2 Kings 2:11) who were taken without suffering physical death. When Christ comes again, the whole generation of Christians who are on earth at that time apparently will bypass physical death and be taken directly to be with God (1 Cor. 15:52; 1 Thess. 4:17).

Jesus, of course, triumphed over death through His resurrection. He promises that someday we will all be resurrected (the unjust as well as the just), and that the "mortal must put on immortality" (1 Cor. 15:53). In other words, someday in the future we will be like Adam in the garden once again. But this will not happen until the end times when Jesus conquers the last of all enemies, death (1 Cor. 15:24-26).

In the meantime, Jesus set the example in doing what He could to relieve physical suffering. He ministered extensively to the poor and showed them His compassion in every way. He cleansed the lepers and gave sight to the blind. He gave His followers the power to heal diseases and to cast out demons. We today are to follow His example. This is especially urgent for those of us who live in affluent societies. We must be concerned for the poor and oppressed and translate our concern into meaningful action. This is not optional behavior for Christians—it is mandatory. That is why I like the term *cultural mandate.*

The spiritual problem. The worst consequence of Adam's sin was spiritual death or separation from God. God originally created Adam in His own image in order to enjoy fellowship. The instant Adam sinned, this fellowship was broken. Instead of being a friend, Adam became God's enemy (Rom. 5:10). Salvation was then needed in the sense of reconciliation to God, and Jesus died on the cross in order to provide that reconciliation (Rom. 5:10). While we were yet sinners, Christ died for us (Rom. 5:8), and we are justified through His blood (Rom. 5:9).

These passages from Romans 5 which we have referred to point out an even more frightening aspect of spiritual death. Verse 9 speaks of our being saved from wrath. Although many people today would like to disguise it, they cannot just wish hell away. Hell is real. It is a place of wrath and torment. Once in hell there is no way out, for hell is the ultimate consequence of sin.

When you think of hell—eternity apart from God with no escape whatsoever—other human problems seem relatively small. Freedom from poverty and fear, racial brotherhood, just social structures, health and well-being—these are all important Kingdom values, but none comes close to being as important as liberation from the wrath to come.

Lost? What's That?

To get back to our original question, then: What do we mean by lost?

Lost materially and socially? Yes.

Lost physically? Yes.

Lost spiritually? Yes, and this is the most serious of all since it carries the possibility that some will be separated from God forever in hell.

When we ask, "Are the heathen lost?" we are essentially asking whether men and women who are not yet committed to Jesus Christ will go to hell. To come straight to the point, the answer is yes, they will. "The wages of sin is death" (Rom. 6:23) just as it was back then in the Garden of Eden. Adam and Eve sinned and died then, people sin and die now.

This brings us to the other half of the verse just quoted (Rom. 6:23): "But the gift of God is eternal life in Jesus Christ our Lord."

We must be crystal clear on this point because it touches on the theological bedrock for missions. Because of sin, every man and every woman is headed for hell, but no one needs to arrive there. The difference between those who arrive and those who do not is Jesus Christ. Those who confess the Lord Jesus and believe in their heart that God raised Him from the dead will be saved (Rom. 10:9). Those who don't, will not. God does not want one person to perish (2 Peter 3:9). This is so important that the angels in heaven rejoice every time a sinner repents of sin and trusts Jesus for salvation (Luke 15:10).

There is no question as to God's desire for everyone to be saved, but how does He carry out His purpose? If He wanted to He could appear face to face with every one of the billions of people in the fourth world, speak to them in their own language, and tell them that Christ died for their sins and that He wants to save them. If God would do this, fine, there would be no need for missions. But He doesn't. Why He doesn't do it this way, all the theologians in Christendom don't know. All we do know is that He has decided to do it in another way. He has decided to use Christian people to take the message of salvation to the lost, and we accept His decision.

The only thing that will save people in the fourth world is faith in Jesus Christ. Romans 10 is a key passage of Scripture for understanding this. It says that "whoever calls upon the name of the Lord shall be saved" (v. 13). From that point on, the logic of the passage is powerful:

How can they call on Him unless they believe in Him?

How can they believe in Jesus if they have never heard of Him?

How can they hear unless someone preaches the gospel to them?

How can anyone go and preach the gospel to them unless he is sent? In its root meaning, *missionary* means a "sent one." That is why Romans 10 is a key missionary passage.

God will save many of those people lost in the fourth world, but He will do it only through men and women who preach to them the gospel of Jesus Christ. This is called the "evangelistic mandate."

Sidestepping the Issue

It is so unpleasant to think of hell as real that some people have attempted to sidestep the issue; they have developed theories of missions that do not require stressing eternal life or eternal damnation. In order to keep it as simple as possible I will call them *universalists* and *horizontalists*, depending upon which approach they take.

Universalists. The doctrine of universalism postulates that all men and women eventually will end up in heaven. Universalists reach this position from several different points of view. Some say that human beings aren't as bad as all that and that they will all somehow make it to heaven. Some say that even if a person does not accept Christ in this life, God will provide other chances in the future until hell is eventually emptied. Some say that if you believe God would permit anyone to stay in hell, you cannot believe that God is love. Some say that we don't know the answer, but we do know that God is a God of grace and that His grace will eventually triumph. Some say that since Christ died on the cross for all, all will be saved.

Universalism is kindly. It is human. It shows deep compassion for men and women, and in this sense it reflects the love of God. But its downfall is that it is not true to the Bible. The Bible does teach that God loves the world (John 3:16) and that Christ died for the sins of the whole world (1 John 2:2). God desires that all be saved and come to the knowledge of the truth (1 Tim. 2:4). But you cannot stop there. You cannot pick and choose which parts of the Bible you like and which you don't like. The Bible is not a divine smorgasbord. You have to take it all, not just what appeals to you.

That means you have to take seriously what Jesus said about the separation of the sheep and the goats and the everlasting fire prepared for the devil and his angels (Matt. 25:31-45). Along with everlasting life, Jesus mentioned everlasting punishment (Matt. 25:46). The gospel is preached so that people will not perish (John 3:16). Those whose names are not written in the Lamb's Book of Life will be cast into the lake of fire (Rev. 20:15).

The Bible calls this the "second death," and describes it in bloodcurdling terms—a lake that burns with fire and brimstone (Rev. 21:8). Whether you interpret this literally or not, it can mean nothing less than horrible suffering. Above all it means separation from God. It is contrasted with the New Jerusalem, and there will be people in each place for eternity.

It is difficult to overstress the danger of universalism. As I survey contemporary mission theology I find evangelical leaders referring to it time and again. George Peters, one of our most respected theologians of missions, calls it "mischievous, unbiblical and unchristian." He says, "It is one of the most serious and pernicious enemies of the Gospel of God and undercuts the nerve of missions more effectively than all other causes combined." Grady Cothen, a high-ranking Southern Baptist leader agrees. He says, "If the church does not believe that men and women are lost, without hope in this world and in the world to come, without Jesus Christ, there is no place for evangelism, and there is no theology of missions."

Universalism is not just a curiosity. Many people believe in it, but they are running away from reality and living in a dreamworld of their own creation. Biblical realism demands that we recognize the painful reality of hell. If we do, the missionary task of the church suddenly takes on tremendously important dimensions.

Horizontalists. Some horizontalists are universalists, but not all of them. Some believe the Bible, but they have come out with what I consider poorly arranged priorities.

What do I mean by *horizontalism*? This is the view that stresses the cultural mandate so much it ends up neglecting the evangelistic mandate. Because human physical and social needs are so immediate and acute, horizontalists focus on them and tend to ignore or downplay human spiritual needs. The horizontal dimension is the person-to-person or the society-to-society relationship. It is contrasted to the vertical which is the relationship of a person to God.

The issue of horizontalism is more complex than universalism. Universalism is essentially an either/or situation. You either believe that lost people who are not saved through Jesus Christ go to hell or you don't. But in the issue raised by horizontalism, you can believe in the urgency of both the cultural mandate and the evangelistic mandate. The question then revolves around the relationship between the two of them.

I like to use a diagram (fig. 1) to clarify this:

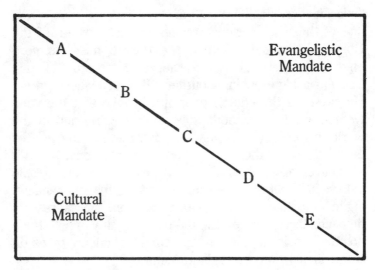

A

Evangelistic
Mandate

B

C

D

Cultural
Mandate

E

Figure 1

If you conceive this as a sliding scale, you can see that a person who adopts the *A* position would say, "I believe only in the cultural mandate." This would be a complete horizontalist. A person at the *E* position would say, "I believe only in the evangelistic mandate." Both are extremes, which in my opinion should be avoided by biblical Christians.

For many years I had the privilege of working closely with John R. W. Stott on the Lausanne Committee. He chaired the Theology Working Group while I chaired the Strategy Working Group. The relationship between the two mandates was one of the major issues we grappled with through much of the seventies. I agree with Stott when he concludes that the word *mission* is properly a comprehensive word. He says, "It therefore includes evangelism and social responsibility, since both are authentic expressions of the love which longs to serve man in his need." So while positions *A* and *E* at the extremes of the scale should be avoided, there are yet any number of positions between them. I have tried to simplify the options by calling them positions *B, C,* and *D.*

Position *B* prioritizes the cultural mandate.

Position *C* considers both the cultural mandate and the evangelistic mandate equal components of mission.

Position *D* prioritizes the evangelistic mandate.

I believe that position *D* is the most consistent with the teaching of the Bible. While we must strive to fulfill both mandates, the evangelistic mandate is primary. Many of my friends disagree with this. Some who tend to be more liberal and follow the theological line, which comes out of the Geneva headquarters of the World Council of Churches, find themselves at position *B.* And some fellow evangelicals, especially those who perceive themselves to be "radical disciples" would hold the *C* position. They call it "holistic evangelism." Why do I disagree?

Go back to the three problems caused by Adam's sin: material and social, physical, and spiritual. The material, social, and physical problems all come under the cultural mandate. The spiritual problems come under the evangelistic mandate. What is God doing, and what does He intend to do about each?

The cultural mandate. God does not intend a total solution to material, social, or physical problems in this life. If He intended a total solution to the material and social lostness of people He would have to remove the cherubim from the gateway to the Garden of Eden, and it looks as though He doesn't intend to do this until the New Jerusalem is ready for occupancy. If he intended a total solution to the physical lostness of people He would banish sickness and death, but He hasn't done this, nor will He until the time of the resurrection when the corruptible shall put on incorruption (1 Cor. 15:53).

In the meantime, the cultural mandate is still in effect. If we are citizens of the Kingdom of God, our life-styles must reflect the values of the Kingdom. We should do all we can to feed the poor, to heal the sick, to comfort the brokenhearted, to liberate the oppressed, and to spread peace upon the earth. This is not optional. But at the same time we must be realistic. God has not made us responsible for bringing in the Kingdom of God in its fullness. Only God will do that at the end of this age. All we do through our social ministry is temporal, not eternal. It is penultimate, not ultimate. It is stopgap, not total.

The evangelistic mandate. Suppose, for the sake of argument, that we successfully fulfilled the cultural mandate but not the evangelistic mandate? Where would that leave us? I agree with Richard Winchell, general director of TEAM mission, who says, "A truly biblical response to social need recognizes that if all who are poor were compensated, if all who are suffering were alleviated, if all who are oppressed were liberated, if all who are ignorant were educated, if all who are hungry were satiated, if all who are deprived were elevated, the world might become a near perfect place. But without the life-transforming power of the gospel, sin would soon be revealed, and the cycle of poverty, suffering, oppression, ignorance, hunger and deprivation would soon be repeated."

Think of this. While God does not offer a total solution to physical and social problems in this life, He does offer such a solution to the spiritual problem here and now. In fact the spiritual problem can be solved *only* in this life. Once a person dies, his spiritual destiny is sealed forever (Heb. 9:27). Solving the spiritual problem then is an ultimate, not a penultimate, issue.

In other words, if you fail to fulfill the cultural mandate it is too bad, but salvation from material, social, and physical lostness will come in the future so long as the ultimate problem is cared for. But if you fail to fulfill the evangelistic mandate you've blown it forever as far as a given person is concerned. That person will never have fellowship with God, and therefore will never enjoy any of the blessings of the New Jerusalem.

No wonder John Stott says, "Is anything so destructive of human dignity as alienation from God through ignorance or rejection of the gospel? And how can we seriously maintain that political and economic liberation is just as important as eternal salvation?"

To the extent that it is reflected in the Lausanne Movement, the evangelical community agrees. The Lausanne Covenant affirms that "in the church's mission of sacrificial service, evangelism is primary." The report from the 1982 Consultation on the Relationship Between Evangelism and Social Responsibility elaborates on this by stating: "Seldom if ever should we have to choose between satisfying physical hunger and spiritual hunger, or between healing bodies and saving souls, since an authentic love for our neighbor will lead us to serve him or her as a whole person. Nevertheless, if we must choose, then we have to say that the supreme and ultimate need of all humankind is the saving grace of Jesus Christ, and that therefore a person's eternal, spiritual salvation is of greater importance than his or her temporal and material well-being."

Put all this together and you see how important missions are. You understand why Jesus said, "Go therefore and make disciples of all the nations, baptizing them in the name of the Father and of the Son and of the Holy Spirit" (Matt. 28:19). You see why missions are not just something for Christians who don't have much else to do; they are the very essence of total obedience to Jesus as Lord.

The heathen *are* lost. They will be lost as long as Christians fail to reach them with the good news of eternal life through Jesus.

But the lost can be found. The sheep can return to the

fold. God's desire is that all be found, and if you're an obedient disciple of Jesus Christ, you will want to be a part of His plan.

Do Something Now!

1. Send $2.00 to Lausanne Committee Publications, Box 1100, Wheaton, Illinois 60189 and ask for a copy of the Lausanne Occasional Paper #21: *Grand Rapids Report: Evangelism and Social Responsibility, An Evangelical Consultation*. This will provide the most up-to-date material available on how the cultural and evangelistic mandates relate to each other in the mission of the church. It will provide stimulating topics for many sessions of a discussion group.

2. Read two excellent and complimentary books on mission theology:

A Biblical Theology of Missions by George W. Peters (Moody Press). This is a complete summary of the classical evangelical position on the missionary task and its implications.

Contemporary Theologies of Mission by Arthur F. Glasser and Donald A. McGavran (Baker Book House). This book, unlike the one above, grapples with the current issues in mission theology which are being raised by both liberals and evangelicals, and argues for the evangelical options.

3. Read *Church Growth and the Whole Gospel* by C. Peter Wagner (Harper & Row Publishers, Inc.). In this book I expand greatly on themes such as the Kingdom of God, our concern for the poor and oppressed, the relationship between the cultural and evangelistic mandates, and many more. This has extensive footnotes which will lead you to numerous other sources if you want to go that deeply into the kinds of issues dealt with in this chapter.

Three
Every Christian Is *Not* A Missionary

I have often heard a stirring missionary message conclude with words to this effect: "Every Christian is a missionary. If you are a Christian you are therefore a missionary. If for some reason you yourself can't go to the mission field, you must send someone in your place!"

This is good rhetoric, but poor theology.

Undoubtedly, this type of appeal has motivated some Christians to take missions more seriously. That is the good news.

But the bad news is that the same appeal has often stimulated two other kinds of reactions which have actually harmed the total cause of missions:

First, some well-meaning Christians have actually gone to the mission field and washed out because they really were not missionaries to start with.

Second, some Christians have not gone to the mission field, but as a result of taking this appeal seriously, they have for many years found themselves plagued by serious and unnecessary guilt feelings, thereby losing part of their Christian joy and reducing the effectiveness of their ministry in other areas.

The notion that every Christian is a missionary, popular as it might be, misconstrues the fundamental nature of the missionary call. To clarify this matter, the most important consideration is understanding the relationship between the missionary call and the biblical doctrine of spiritual gifts. The purpose of this chapter, then, is to attempt to fit the missionary call into the total biblical teaching on spiritual gifts. I want to explain clearly what the missionary gift is, and thereby help you to see just where God has placed you in the total picture.

God says He does not want us to be ignorant of spiritual gifts (1 Cor. 12:1). He wants us to: (a) know the doctrine of spiritual gifts, and (b) know exactly where each one of us fits in.

Ignorance of spiritual gifts apparently was one of the serious problems of the Corinthian church (Paul dedicated chapters 12, 13, and 14 of 1 Corinthians to the subject). Unfortunately, such ignorance continues to retard some of our churches today. Many people, however, are waking up to the need to understand and apply biblical teaching on spiritual gifts to their lives and to their churches. Among some it is becoming a very strong emphasis, whereas a decade or two ago the same Christians may have been exceedingly timid about the subject. Even during my own seminary training in the early 1950s my professors implied that many of the gifts had ceased at the end of the apostolic age. One reason for this attitude was that these professors, like many others, had not yet come to terms with the Pentecostal movement which, at that time, had not gained the strength and acceptance it enjoys today. Some people avoided stressing spiritual gifts for fear that someone might classify them as Pentecostals. But fortunately the situation is changing.

One of the first non-Pentecostal churches to recognize and practice the dynamic of spiritual gifts was Peninsula Bible Church under the leadership of Pastor Ray Stedman. His book *Body Life,* published in the early seventies, helped many of us who were not Pentecostals or charismatics open up to the biblical teaching on the gifts. When I became a missionary back in the mid-fifties, few mission agencies, if any at all, accepted, rejected, or even placed candidates on the basis of spiritual gifts. Now a large number of them are very specific about spiritual gifts in their personnel recruitment process.

But despite these encouraging signs, much ignorance of spiritual gifts yet persists.

What Spiritual Gifts Are Not

Before attempting to understand just what spiritual gifts are, it will help to clarify what they are not, particularly in two areas:

Spiritual gifts are not natural talents. Every member of the human race has some sort of natural talent. Your natural talent may or may not carry over and become your spiritual gift. It is common, for example, for a person who is a good teacher before becoming a Christian to discover the spiritual gift of teaching after conversion. But this is not necessarily the case.

When a person becomes a Christian and his name is written in the Lamb's Book of Life, he receives a spiritual gift. In other words, every Christian without exception has a spiritual gift (1 Cor. 12:7). This is natural because becoming a Christian involves becoming a member of the Body of Christ, and God expects every member of the

Body to function. Each Christian functions basically according to his or her spiritual gift.

No one has a spiritual gift *before* conversion, although he undoubtedly has natural talents. Every Christian has one or more gifts *after* conversion. Of course they keep their natural talents as well. The problem is that many Christians do not realize they have a spiritual gift, and therefore they either do not use it or they use it by accident, so to speak. No wonder some of our churches are impotent. The members of the Body are not working effectively. They are suffering paralysis. Some pastors attempt to remedy the problem by souping up their church programs; but like iron lungs, many such programs are artificial support systems. What is really needed for spiritual vitality in our churches is a massive awakening of Christians to their spiritual gifts.

I am convinced that more than enough spiritual power to win the world in our generation is now bottled up in existing churches, but it will be released only when Christians realize that they are members of the Body and begin working at it.

Spiritual gifts are not fruit of the Spirit. One of the most common misstatements made by Christians is to speak of the "gift of love." Biblically, love is not classified as a spiritual gift, but rather as a fruit of the Spirit. Galatians 5:22 says, "The *fruit* of the Spirit is love, joy, peace . . . "

You will be confused if you do not realize that whereas not all Christians have the same *gifts*, all must exhibit the same *fruit*, namely love and its derivatives. This is precisely why 1 Corinthians 13, the great love chapter of the Bible, is an integral part of a key passage on gifts, 1 Corinthians 12-14. The first three verses of chapter 13 name several of the spiritual gifts and go on to say that you can have the gifts, but without love (fruit) these gifts are sounding brass and a tinkling cymbal—they profit nothing

(1 Cor. 13:1-3). One reason the Corinthian church was in such a disastrous condition when Paul wrote was that they had all the gifts (1 Cor. 1:7), but they lacked the fruit.

Gifts and fruit are like an engine and wheels. You can have a roaring engine, but without wheels the car won't go. The wheels alone can roll downhill, but not much more. Cars need both engine and wheels. The church needs both spiritual gifts and the fruit of the Spirit.

Notice that there is no direct relationship between a person's sanctification (meaning growth in grace, Christian maturity, walk with the Lord, or whatever you might call it) and the *possession* of spiritual gifts. If you are a Christian you will have spiritual gifts whether you have much fruit of the Spirit or not. But there is a direct relationship between *effectiveness* in the use of the gifts you have and the quality of your Christian life. Only when the Holy Spirit is in control of your life and the fruit of the Spirit is there can you use your gifts for the glory of God.

What the Spiritual Gifts Are

The three major lists of spiritual gifts are found in 1 Corinthians 12, Romans 12, and Ephesians 4. There is some overlapping in the lists, but each one adds something new. Put them all together and you come out with a composite something like this:

Administration	Knowledge
Apostle	Leadership
Discerning of Spirits	Mercy
Evangelist	Miracles
Exhortation	Pastor
Faith	Prophecy
Giving	Service
Healing	Teaching
Helps	Tongues
Interpretation	Wisdom

Of course, at this point it would be interesting to stop and define each one of these gifts, but I have done that in my book *Your Spiritual Gift Can Help Your Church Grow*, so I will not go into that much detail here. At the moment we are basically concerned as to just where the *missionary* fits into the total picture.

In order to do that, we must first notice that none of the three major lists of gifts is exhaustive. There is no reason to think the composite list above is exhaustive, either. For one thing, other gifts pop up outside the main lists. They include the gift of celibacy (1 Cor. 7:7), the gifts of martyrdom and voluntary poverty (1 Cor. 13:3), the gift of hospitality (1 Pet. 4:9), and the missionary gift which I will explain in detail later.

Gifts and Roles

We have already distinguished between gifts and natural talents and between gifts and fruit. At this point it will help to distinguish between gifts and *roles*.

If you go back over the list of spiritual gifts you will notice that several of them do not seem to describe anything particularly special at all. They simply name things that all Christians are expected to do.

Take, for example, the gift of faith. What Christian doesn't have faith? But when you examine it a little closer you find that there are at least three kinds of faith mentioned in the New Testament.

Saving faith. "By grace you have been saved through *faith*, and that not of yourselves; it is the gift of God" (Eph. 2:8, italics added). When a person becomes a Christian he or she receives the gift of saving faith. Therefore every Christian has this kind of faith, but it is not to be confused with the other kinds.

Faith as fruit of the Spirit. "The fruit of the Spirit is

love, joy, peace, longsuffering, gentleness, goodness, *faith* . . . " (Gal. 5:22, *KJV*; italics added). Every Christian's life should be characterized by a constant attitude of faith, produced by the presence of the Holy Spirit. This kind of faith is what I call a *role,* something expected of every Christian. In that sense it is different from a *gift.*

The gift of faith (1 Cor. 12:9). As in the case of other gifts, some Christians have a special ability to exercise faith that other Christians don't have. In one place in the Scriptures it is described as "faith . . . to remove mountains" (1 Cor. 13:2). George Müeller of Bristol is a well-known model of someone with this gift. Contemporary leaders such as Bill Bright, Robert Schuller, and Ralph Winter have this gift.

Giving or liberality (Rom. 12:8) is another example of the difference between gift and role. Giving is not an optional activity for a Christian. Every Christian is expected to give to the Lord's work as a matter of course. In fact, it is my opinion that if you give less than 10 percent of your income you are robbing God. You are not fulfilling your *role.* But over and above that, some Christians have a remarkable *gift* of liberal giving. One Christian business-man with this gift used to donate 90 percent of his income to God's work, and then tithe his own 10 percent! As every fully supported missionary knows, such people are crucial in God's kingdom, but it is not expected that every Christian can or will give that large a proportion of his income. Only those with the gift of liberality will do it properly and consistently.

The Gifts and the Body

If you check it out you'll notice that in every one of the three Bible passages where a major list of spiritual gifts appears (1 Cor. 12; Rom. 12; Eph. 4) Paul uses the analogy of the body. Instead of simply saying that "Christians are members of the church," he puts it much more graphically: "Christians are members of the body of Christ." This is good. Back then not many people knew what the Church was. Today too many people may know what it is, and some have consequently developed weird ideas as to just what the Church is and what its members are supposed to do.

But the human body is the same now as it was then, and the average person has a basic knowledge of the body and its members. You don't have to be able to describe cloning or have a degree in anatomy to understand how hands, eyes, veins, knees, and skin relate to one another in daily life. The analogy spans time and cultures. Eskimo teeth are used to masticate food just like Korean or Arab teeth. Breasts nourish babies from Argentina to Zaire. When you ask almost any human being to think of Christians as members of the body, he can follow the analogy easily.

With a minimum of explanation, people understand that the body is one organism. In three ways this is particularly related to the Church:

The body has one head. The brain controls the central nervous system and provides direction and coordination to the whole body. In this sense, Christ is the Head of the Body of Christ (Eph. 4:15-16). Regardless of the gifts one might have, no Christian should get the idea that he or she is head of the Body. Jesus is, and Jesus alone.

The body has one blood. Every cell of the human body receives nourishment from the same blood. The drop of blood that feeds the calf of my leg this time might feed my earlobe the next time around. The Body of Christ is also nourished by one blood. Every true Christian has been brought into the Body through the blood of Christ (Eph. 1:7), and no other way.

The body has one spirit. The human soul or spirit is

unconfined. The same spirit is in your thumb or your bone marrow or your gall bladder. It cannot be isolated into one member only. By the same token, the Holy Spirit is in every member of the Body of Christ (Rom. 8:9).

These three powerful factors unify the body; nevertheless the members differ one from another. How do the gifts get there? The Bible clearly says that they are placed there by the Holy Spirit Himself (1 Cor. 12:11,18). Every Christian's spiritual gift makes him or her a particular member of the Body, and that gift is given entirely by God's choice. It is a mistake to think that God gives us a celestial order blank with a list of the gifts and invites us to check off the ones we would like best. Some verses that might sound like that (such as "desire the best gifts" or "desire spiritual gifts" as in 1 Cor. 12:31 and 14:1) refer not to the individual Christian but to the church in general. No other person, whether pastor or teacher or archbishop, can pass out spiritual gifts to fellow Christians. God uses men and women to do some things for Him, but this task is not one of them. He does it "as He wills" (1 Cor. 12:11).

The reason for this is that the worldwide Church is such a complex organism that only God Himself has a broad enough grasp of the Church and its needs to distribute the gifts properly. Since God is in charge, it does not seem possible that any church would lack the gifts it needs to function in a healthy and vital way. Sick and ineffective churches probably do not lack the gifts; their members simply are not using them as they should.

Just as God gives different gifts to different people, He also gives different combinations of gifts to different churches. This is why I don't get nervous just because my own local church does not have exactly the same gifts as the church down the street. God knows what gifts each of us needs to function properly. But in spite of this diversity, gifts must be used together, coordinated by the Head. Jesus must be fully in charge. My foot is working well now, but if I cut it off and put it over on the couch, it might still be my foot (no one else would claim it!), but it is of no use to me because the head could no longer control it.

All members of the Body need each other. Make believe you see a peanut vendor down the street. Now make a list of every member of your body that you need in order to buy a sack of peanuts, eat one, and nourish your body with its protein. That's why Paul says, "The eye cannot say to the hand, 'I have no need of you'" (1 Cor. 12:21). No matter what my own gifts are, they are useless unless they are working with other members of the Body.

Where You Fit In

So much for what could be called the biblical doctrine of spiritual gifts. But as I mentioned previously, not only does God want us to know the doctrine, He also wants us to know how each one of us fits into the practical working out of the doctrine.

This practical side is vitally important to every Christian because it relates so closely to the final judgment. It is no news that someday each Christian is going to appear before Christ for his judgment (2 Cor. 5:10). Some will be called a "good and faithful servant," but others will be "wicked and lazy servant," according to the parable in Matthew 25:14-30.

What will be the basis of judgment? Obviously, what you and I did with what God entrusted to us. He entrusts many things to us to use in this life, but nothing is more important than the spiritual gifts He gives us. To a large extent, then, we will be judged according to how we function as members of the Body of Christ during our life on earth. A Christian who doesn't take the time, effort, and prayer necessary to be sure of his or her own particular gift or gifts will not be well prepared for the judgment. That is one reason why God does not want us ignorant of spiritual gifts (1 Cor. 12:1).

Notice the vital relationship between the judgment verse (2 Cor. 5:10) and the major spiritual gift passage (Rom. 12). Second Corinthians says we will be judged according to what we did in our *bodies,* good or bad. Romans says we must present our *bodies* a living sacrifice. How do we do this, proving the good, acceptable, and perfect will of God? Romans 12:1-2 are only the introductory verses to the passage that follows on the Body and the gifts (Rom. 12:3-8).

In order to please God, then, I need to know what my gift is, or as Paul says, I need to "think soberly, as God hath dealt to each one a measure of faith" (Rom. 12:3). I must avoid the extremes of being either too proud or too humble, and I must go through whatever spiritual exercise is necessary in order to come to an accurate and realistic conclusion as to what gift God has given me and to what degree I have it. On that basis I live my Christian life and function as a member of the Body of Christ.

Know What Your Gift Isn't

Just as important as knowing what gift God *has* given you is knowing which gifts He *hasn't* given you. Many Christians try for years to function with gifts they never had in the first place, and this doesn't do the Lord's work much good. It's like trying to hear something with your knee or throw a ball with your nose. Knees and noses are better off doing other things.

No one told me this while I was in seminary, and consequently, when I first went to Bolivia as a missionary, I had the idea that I wanted to be an evangelist like Billy Graham. But after some time I became concerned that in spite of well-constructed and thoroughly biblical evangelistic sermons, when I gave the invitation, no one would come! For a long time I worried that I wasn't praying enough, or that some sin in my life was standing between me and God, or that I needed more of the Holy Spirit or the deeper life. I worked on these problems diligently, but to no avail. I still gave invitations and nobody came! Personal evangelism produced similar results, and very few came to Christ through my evangelistic ministry.

Whenever I thought of Billy Graham I became more and more frustrated. When he held out his arms and said, "Come!" multitudes came. I held out *my* arms almost in vain.

Then the Lord showed me what I am now sharing about spiritual gifts. Among other things, He showed me that I did not have the gift of evangelist. This was a turning point in my Christian life. Frustrations and guilt lifted like the morning mist. I began to feel a joy in serving Christ I had not experienced before. I now know that I am not another Billy Graham. God has given him the gift of evangelist, but He has not given it to me. I still receive occasional invitations to preach evangelistic crusades, but I turn them down without hesitation. Life is too short to squander my energies attempting to be something I now know I am not.

Let me hasten to add that I still have a *role* as a witness, and I try to be faithful in this. God occasionally gives me the privilege of leading a soul to Christ, and when I do it is a red-letter day for me. But I also realize that the *role* of a witness is not the same as the *gift* of an evangelist.

I have experimented with other gifts, such as the gift of pastor, with a similar lack of results. On the positive side, God has showed me what gifts I *do* have. I have three in particular—knowledge, teacher, and missionary—and I spend a very large part of my waking hours using these three gifts with all the vigor I can muster.

When the time comes for the judgment, Jesus is not going to ask me what I have done with the gifts of an evangelist or a pastor, since He never gave them to me. But He *is* going to ask me what I did as a scholar, teacher, and missionary, and I want to be ready for His questions.

If you come to "think soberly of yourself" in this light, you will avoid three very common spiritual pitfalls.

First, false pride. Since God is the one who assigns the gifts and consequent functions as a member of the Body, your gift is in no way of your own making. You have no reason at all to be proud of it or to consider yourself superior to any other person (or member of the Body).

Second, false humility. If you carry the Christian virtue of humility too far you may find yourself saying, "I am just a tiny member of the Body, and my gifts don't amount to much. Others may be giants, but I am satisfied to be a nobody." Result: You think you have no gift, and you do nothing. This false humility is detrimental to your own life and to the Body as a whole. Just be honest and realistic about what God has given you and don't be afraid to admit you have a gift.

Third, envy. When you look around, there will be others who *do* appear to be giants. God has placed each one in his or her proper place, however, and this includes you. God wants you to be happy with the gift you have, happy with the gifts others have, and happy to be able to work together for His glory. Just the thought of an eyelid envying a fingernail because it does different things is ridiculous. None of us should envy either those with gifts different from ours or those with a greater measure of the same gift.

How to Find Your Gift

By now you may agree with me that one of the most important spiritual exercises that a Christian can possibly undertake is a sincere and relentless search for his or her own spiritual gift or gifts. To conclude this section I will suggest five steps that you should take to do this. If you get a positive response to all five, you can be reasonably sure that you have the gift involved.

First, explore the options. Know what the gifts are and what they imply. This chapter has been a starter, particularly for the missionary gift. Study well 1 Corinthians 12, Romans 12, and Ephesians 4. Read other books.

Second, experiment with as many as possible. You won't be able to try out every gift on the list, but you can try many, as I tried the gifts of pastor and evangelist.

Third, examine your own feelings about the gift you are experimenting with. I believe that God wants happy Christians, and if He has given you a gift He will give you unusual joy when you are using it. You ought to feel better about being able to use your gift than you do about almost any other activity you can think of.

Fourth, evaluate your effectiveness. Your gift should accomplish what it was intended for. If you are a teacher, others will learn. If you are an evangelist, others will come to Christ. This is just as natural as expecting your nose to smell.

Fifth, expect confirmation from the Body. If you have the gift, others in the Body will recognize it. This is essential, since every gift must be used with the other members. Ordination to the ministry is one way a gift is validated, but fellow Christians should confirm every gift, not just that of pastor. There are no Lone Rangers when it comes to spiritual gifts.

Once you find your gift, take all the time necessary to (a) develop the gift, and (b) use the gift. If you do this, without forgetting that it must be used in combination with the fruit of the Spirit, you can expect to hear, "Well done, good and faithful servant" on that final day.

The Missionary Gift

By now it should be clearer why I said up front that every Christian is *not* a missionary. The reason is simply that not every Christian has the missionary gift. The Bible says that the whole body cannot be an eye because if it were it couldn't hear (1 Cor. 12:17). If every Christian were a missionary, where would be the pastors, the evangelists, the counselors, the teachers, and the prophets? As a matter of fact, a relatively small minority of believers has the missionary gift.

Before I explain further, let me define what I mean by the missionary gift. The missionary gift is the special ability that God gives to certain members of the Body of Christ to minister whatever other spiritual gifts they have in a second culture. It is the specific gift of cross-cultural ministry.

There are two frequent areas of confusion which need to be clarified before the missionary gift can be fully understood:

First, don't confuse the missionary gift with the gift of apostle. The gift of apostle is the special ability that God gives to certain members of the Body of Christ to assume and exercise general leadership over a number of churches with extraordinary authority in spiritual matters which is spontaneously recognized and appreciated by those churches. Apostles often have the gifts of evangelist and teacher as well. But in order to function as an apostle, it is not necessary to minister in a second culture. Some apostles are also missionaries and do minister in second cultures, but some apostles do not have the missionary gift and they minister mostly in their own culture.

Peter was an example of an apostle without the missionary gift. He made short excursions into other cultures, such as to the house of Cornelius, to the Samaritans, and to Antioch. But he was known as the "apostleship to the circumcised" (Gal. 2:8). He was a Jew ministering to fellow Jews.

On the other hand, Paul was an example of an apostle who also had the gift of missionary. He was called to minister in another culture, a Jew to Gentiles. The Scripture portion that explains how God did this in Paul's life is Ephesians 3:1-9. There Paul speaks of himself as the prisoner of Jesus Christ for the Gentiles (3:1). He was a Hebrew through and through (Acts 22:3; 23:6), and to identify closely with pork-eating Gentiles was not at all natural for him. But Paul says he was made a minister to the Gentiles "according to the gift of the grace of God" (Eph. 3:7). He emphasizes that his ability to preach to the Gentiles was from the "grace . . . given" (Eph. 3:8), which gains meaning when we realize that the word *grace* is synonymous with *spiritual gifts* (Rom. 12:6).

In other words, Paul's spiritual gift enabled him to minister in another culture. The best statement of what this missionary gift does is in 1 Cor. 9:22 where Paul says, "I have become all things to all men, that I might by all means save some." Not everyone can do it. Peter, for example, couldn't. That's why Paul says clearly, "The gospel for the uncircumcised [Gentiles] had been committed to me, as the gospel of the circumcised [Jews] was to Peter" (Gal. 2:7). If we adopt the hypothesis of the missionary gift, all these pieces fall into place.

Just having the missionary gift doesn't guarantee that a person will be a good missionary, but it increases the probability considerably. It helps the person learn the new language and culture. It reduces (but never eliminates) the effects of culture shock. I know missionaries who have been on the field for ten or twenty years and still have culture shock. This is an obvious sign to me that they don't have the missionary gift.

Second, don't confuse the missionary gift with the gift of evangelist. The gift of evangelist is the special ability that God gives to certain members of the Body of Christ to share the gospel with unbelievers in such a way that they become Jesus' disciples and responsible members of the Body of Christ. Every Christian has the role of being a good witness, but not every one has the gift of evangelist. Some missionaries have the gift of evangelist, and some do not. Those who do not may have the gift of teaching or mercy or exhortation or healing or service or whatever.

I am one of them. As I explained earlier, I first thought I was going to be the Billy Graham of Bolivia. Then I discovered that God had not given me the gift of evangelist. But I also discovered that I did have the gift of teaching. Because I had the gift of missionary as well, I was able to use my gift of teaching effectively in a second culture. But I no longer confuse the gift of missionary with the gift of evangelist.

The Gift and the Call

Very frequently a person will say, "I think I am called to be a missionary." What exactly is the "call"? How does the call relate to the missionary gift?

To come right to the point, there is essentially no difference between the call and the gift. If God gives you a missionary gift, He also calls you to use it for His glory. If He calls you to be a missionary, He will give you the gift you need for the job.

But there is another sense in which we can understand "call." Suppose you do have the missionary gift. You need some kind of indication as to just where God wants you to use the gift. In a real sense, then, God may call you to India or to evangelize Muslims, or to urban ministry. While he was in Troas, God called the apostle Paul and his group to Philippi through the Macedonian vision, "Come over and help us."

You may not have the missionary gift. Chances are you don't. Research I have done has indicated that probably less than 1 percent of biblical Christians have the missionary gift. This may sound extremely low, but it isn't. If 1 percent of the forty million evangelicals in the United States were activated as missionaries, we would have 400 thousand missionaries. As it is, we have only around fifty thousand. With 400 thousand missionaries from the United States, plus an equivalent number of workers from churches in other countries, there would be no shortage of personnel to undertake and complete the task of reaching the 16,750 people groups in the world yet to have the gospel introduced to them.

But if you are part of the majority of Christians who do not have the missionary gift, you are nevertheless expected to be a world Christian. That is the role which corresponds to this gift. I like the way David Bryant defines world Christian in his book *In the Gap*: "World Christians are day-to-day disciples for whom Christ's global cause has become the integrating, overriding priority for all that He is for them."

How do you know if you have the missionary gift? Go back over the five steps for discovering your spiritual gift that I outlined earlier in this chapter. A good first step, if your life situation permits it, is to undertake a short-term missionary service. You can sign up with a mission agency and go out to work in another culture for terms of three months upward. Ordinarily, a year is regarded as the minimum for really discovering whether you have the missionary gift and are being called to make a career of it. Shorter periods of time hardly give you a chance to move past the tourist stage of involvement. Two years is probably ideal. Since this is a period of experimentation, you need to pray for yourself and have other Christian friends support you in prayer so that God will make His will clear to you during your time of service. You will not be alone. The *MARC Handbook* estimates that there are around eighty-five hundred North American short termers serving overseas at any given time.

Do Something Now!

1. Read *Your Spiritual Gifts Can Help Your Church Grow* by C. Peter Wagner (Regal Books). Of all the books I have written, this by far has been the most helpful to people in their own personal spiritual life. I think it will help you also if you are serious about finding what spiritual gift or gifts God has given you.

2. Send $2.00 to the Charles E. Fuller Institute of Evangelism and Church Growth, Box 989, Pasadena, California 91102 and request a copy of the "Modified Houts Questionnaire." This self-administered questionnaire of 125 questions will help you know yourself better and give you a good start toward gift discovery. Ask the Fuller Institute also for information on their spiritual gifts workshop package, a group discovery program which I helped develop some years ago and which has benefited hundreds of churches.

3. Write to the Institute for American Church Growth, 150 S. Los Robles Avenue, Suite 600, Pasadena, California 91101 and ask for information on their self-study spiritual gifts package called "Spiritual Gifts for Building the Body." If you decide to get involved in this excellent study, you will need to set aside twenty-five to thirty hours of time, and you will be greatly enriched.

Four

How the Machinery of Missions Runs

It is reported that every year over $1 billion is spent on missions by people in the United States and Canada.

This substantial enterprise is supported almost entirely by voluntary contributions from Christians. Millions of Americans support the missionary work of the church, but relatively few of them understand how these missions work, what the different options are, and how they can track their dollars to see if they are accomplishing the intended goals.

Are Missions an Afterthought?

The word *missions* is commonly used in two senses. It often means the "missionary enterprise" of the church as a whole, or the composite of the efforts that Christians make to spread the gospel of Christ throughout the world.

This is the most general meaning of the word. That is how I use it when I say that I teach in a school of "missions."

A more specific meaning of the word often refers to missionary organizations or groups which have been formed in one way or another as agencies for carrying out the larger missionary enterprise. When I raise the question in this section, "Are missions an afterthought?" I mean missions in this organizational sense.

Mission agencies have now become a primary instrument for world evangelization, as we will see. But before describing some of the details as to their machinery, we need to feel comfortable about their existence. Some people believe that missionary agencies are abnormal. They say that not missions but the churches themselves are the instruments God really wants to use for extending His Kingdom. One recent writer calls the development of autonomous missionary societies an "unfortunate and abnormal historic development." Some look at missionary societies as warts on the fair skin of the church, and the sooner we can remove them the better.

I disagree!

I see missions as intrinsically related to the church—not as abnormalities but something like legs which are related to the body.

In one sense the word *church* is so general that it includes everything we are talking about. The Church universal (sometimes called the "invisible church") includes every Christian and every group of Christians on the earth. In that sense, local churches, missionary societies, summer Bible camps, theological seminaries, Bible societies, and whatever other Christian activity you might name are all part of the church. This is correct, but it is not very helpful at this point.

What we mean specifically by *church* is a particular, visible organization. We are talking about a *congregational structure.* It could be a local congregation, an association of churches, a whole denomination like the United Presbyterian Church, or even a state church like the Anglican Church in England.

There are some notable exceptions to the rule, but throughout history churches *as churches* have not been particularly effective instruments for carrying the gospel to the regions beyond. The outstanding success stories in world evangelization have usually come from situations in which the church or churches have permitted, encouraged, and supported the formation of specialized *mission structures* to do their missionary work.

The Roman Catholic Church learned this lesson through the centuries. Early on, they discovered the value of mission structures. Those of our own ancestors who inhabited the forests of northern Europe were largely won to Christ through missionaries working in what is called the monastic movement. The Benedictine order was founded around A.D. 500 and it was influential through Augustine of Canterbury in the conversion of England. The Franciscans, founded in the thirteenth century, sent missionaries to China and many other parts of the world. While the missionary movement of the churches of the Protestant Reformation was zero in the sixteenth century, the Jesuit order was formed in France to carry Christianity throughout the world. Today, 75 percent of Roman Catholic missionary work is done by the orders and only 25 percent by the local clergy. Of 6,393 Catholic missionaries sent out from the U.S. in 1980, only 3 percent were sent out by dioceses.

The Protestant Reformation movement of the sixteenth century was slow to catch on to the structural facts of life. One of Martin Luther's blind spots was that he reacted so strongly against the corrupt aspects of the monastic movement (he belonged to the Augustinian

Order) that he failed to appreciate what they were doing well. It did not occur to him to reform Catholic *missions* while he was reforming the Catholic *church*. So the Protestant Reformation movement ended up all congregational structure and no mission structure. There is no doubt that Luther himself desired that the gospel should be carried throughout the whole earth. Luther sharpened the missionary *message,* but with all his brilliance he never came clear on missionary *structures.* He was primarily a theologian and a churchman, not a missionary.

Luther was not able to see that using mission structures for the spread of the gospel seems to have been God's plan all along. The biblical model for missionary structures is the Pauline band, first formed in Antioch and then used to carry the gospel throughout the first-century world. Acts 13:1-3 describes its organization. Many, when they read the passage, assume at first glance that the Antioch church itself sent out the missionaries. But a closer study shows that this is not necessarily so. The five persons named in Acts 13:1 (Barnabas, Simeon, Lucius, Manaen, and Saul) were outsiders who had been called in to help the church, but none of them so far as we know was either a longtime resident of Antioch or a member of the congregations there. They were prophets and teachers who related to the church much as missionaries relate to a national church today. When the Holy Spirit told them that Saul and Barnabas were to move on, the other three laid hands on them and they went forth. The event described in Acts 13 was more than likely a mission structure activity, not a congregational structure activity.

Paul's missionary band increased in number as the years went by, and from the data we have it seems that Paul himself functioned as the general director and coordinator. He reported back to Antioch from time to time, just as he reported to Jerusalem and the other churches. The church in Philippi most likely was one of the financial supporters of the mission. But the missionary society was not controlled by Antioch or Jerusalem or Philippi, so far as we can determine. The church was the church, and the mission was the mission, right from the beginning.

The great Protestant missionary movement began only when the heirs of Luther, Calvin, and Zwingli stumbled onto the importance of the missionary society. This happened as one of the results of the great Evangelical Awakening of the 1700s led by John and Charles Wesley and George Whitefield. Missionary societies were not unknown, since the Society for the Propagation of the Gospel in Foreign Parts had been founded in England as early as 1701, but that group was interested largely in ministry to British citizens overseas. The real turning point came in the years 1795-1815 when scores of what were called "voluntary associations" were formed. One of the models for these was the Baptist Missionary Society, which came into being in 1792 through the vision of William Carey, now known as the father of modern missions. The first one in the United States was the American Board of Commissioners for Foreign Missions, which Congregationalists and others established in New England in 1810.

Once missionary societies gained strength, wonderful things began to happen. More men and women have been led to Christ and more Christian churches have been planted in the world in the 190 years since William Carey than in the eighteen hundred previous years all put together. Missions, then, are not an afterthought. They are not God's "Plan B." They are an integral part of His design for "making disciples of all nations."

Missions are not warts on the church, they are legs. The body can survive without legs, but it can't get around well. The church can survive without missions (as the churches of the Reformation did), but they can't do a good job of proclaiming Christ's name throughout the world. Legs move the body, and the body nourishes and sustains the legs. Missions move the church out, and the church in turn sustains missions. As legs are distinct, yet a part of the body, so missions are a part of the church—but don't confuse their specific functions.

What Missionary Societies Look Like

Some years ago Ralph Winter introduced the technical term *modality* to describe the congregational structure, which includes entire families regardless of age or sex. *Sodality* is the term that describes the mission structure or voluntary association which only those particularly interested in the stated task of the group join and participate in. Modalities and sodalities are not mutually exclusive, they need each other. Catholic orders such as the Jesuits and Maryknoll Fathers are mission structures, but they operate within one congregational structure, the Catholic Church. The Anglican Church also has such mission structures as the Church Missionary Society or the South America Missionary Society. The World Mission Prayer League is a Lutheran mission that relates to several different Lutheran churches in the U.S.A. The Sudan Interior Mission is another type of mission structure, relating to churches of all denominations but almost exclusively to those of evangelical persuasion. Some denominations such as the United Presbyterian Church have discouraged the formation of semi-autonomous mission structures. They prefer to run their mission program through a church board called the Program Agency.

A less scientific but more common terminology to describe certain kinds of missions is *denominational* and *interdenominational*. The members of a *denominational mission* come from the same denomination, and when they go to the mission field they plant churches of that denomination. Examples are the Southern Baptist Foreign Mission Board, Assemblies of God Division of Foreign Missions, and the World Division of the Board of Global Ministries of the United Methodist Church.

Interdenominational missions, also called *faith missions,* get their support from a variety of sources, recruit members without regard to their denominational affiliation, and often form a new, local denomination when they successfully plant churches on the mission field.

Three of the largest interdenominational missions which plant churches on the field are The Evangelical Alliance Mission (TEAM), Sudan Interior Mission (SIM) International, and Africa Inland Mission (AIM). Examples of others which do not plant churches but undertake various tasks contributing toward world evangelization are Wycliffe Bible Translators, Youth with a Mission, and Mission Aviation Fellowship.

One of the more recent trends is for a few of the agencies to have larger numbers of missionaries. A full half of all North American Protestant missionaries belong to only fifteen mission agencies. In recent years several interdenominational missions have merged in order to cut down on overhead and management expenses.

Associations of Missions

Although some giant missions like the Southern Baptists, Wycliffe Bible Translators, and New Tribes Mission have chosen not to join any of the major associations of missions in the United States, most of the missions have. The five most important U.S. associations of agencies are as follows:

1. *Division of Overseas Ministries, National Council of Churches.* Generally speaking, the DOM brings together what are known as the mainline denominations. It has a

membership of thirty-two missions representing just under five thousand missionaries, less than half from NCC denominations. Income approaches $200 million annually.

2. *Interdenominational Foreign Mission Association.* Organized in 1917, the IFMA represents ninety interdenominational mission boards, all evangelical in persuasion, representing roughly ten thousand seven-hundred missionaries. Income is about $150 million.

3. *Evangelical Foreign Missions Association.* Affiliated with the National Association of Evangelicals, the EFMA includes mostly denominational missions, but several interdenominational missions also hold membership, some jointly with IFMA. The membership totals eighty-two missions, representing more than ten thousand missionaries. Income is $350 million.

The IFMA and the EFMA work closely together on many projects, and are presently cooperating in five joint committees. One of them, Evangelical Missions Information tion Service, publishes the influential journal, *Evangelical Missions Quarterly,* the *Missionary News Service,* and several area editions of *Pulse.*

4. *The Associated Missions of the International Council of Christian Churches.* TAM represents six missions, with a total missionary force of about 200. Income is $2.5 million. Its members are generally congenial to the leadership of Carl McIntire.

5. *The Fellowship of Missions.* The five members of the FOM are fundamentalist in outlook, and their missionary force totals about twelve hundred with a cumulative budget of over $18 million. Some denominations, such as the General Association of Regular Baptists, do not run their own denominational missionary program, but have approved these five mission agencies (which include Baptist organizations such as Baptist Mid-Missions and the Association of Baptists for World Evangelism) as their offi-

cial missionary arms or, to follow the previous analogy, their legs.

An analysis of associations of missions reveals some significant recent trends. For one thing, the agencies representing the ecumenically-minded mainline Protestant denominations have been in general decline since the sixties. Over all there has been a noticeable shift in missionary personnel and funding from these groups to the more evangelically-oriented missions. For instance, during the decade of the seventies, the DOM (the more liberal group) lost 3,462 missionaries, while the IFMA and EFMA (the more evangelical groups) gained 3,785. Income-wise, the DOM increased by $28 million or 24 percent while the IFMA/EFMA increased by $285 million or 293 percent.

Another significant trend is the rapidly increasing strength of the unaffiliated agencies. Ten years ago the associations of agencies represented two-thirds of the Protestant missionary force. Now the total is under one-half and decreasing. This can be attributed both to the vigorous growth of large unaffiliated agencies such as Southern Baptists, New Tribes Mission, and Wycliffe Bible Translators and to the proliferation of new smaller agencies which choose to remain independent of the rest.

A Variety of Functions

Most missions are in the business of preaching the gospel, bringing men and women to a commitment to Christ, and planting Christian churches wherever they go. It is fitting that the majority do this, since the evangelistic mandate is primary in missions. But other kinds of missions have been formed for other objectives. In fact, the *MARC Handbook* has a section in which all mission agencies are listed by their primary task. In this section there are no less than 118 headings, from adoption programs and agricultural assistance to workshops for nationals and youth ministry. Some of the major categories of mission agencies which are not primarily engaged in evangelizing and planting or nurturing churches would include education, literature, humanitarian ministries, service and/or support, media and medical.

Service missions specialize in certain tasks which they perform to aid a wide variety of other missions, but they themselves do not specialize in evangelism and church planting. Mission Aviation Fellowship, for example, provides air transportation for scores of missions that are in no position to operate their own flying program. Daystar Communications offers technical training in communications to church leaders around the world. Gospel Recordings presses and distributes records carrying evangelistic messages in hundreds of vernacular languages. The United Bible Societies translate, print and distribute the Scriptures in multiple languages. The list could go on and on.

Some mission agencies have little or no personnel overseas. The Christian Nationals' Evangelism Commission (CNEC), for example, was founded with the purpose of raising funds to support the ministry of selected national leaders in the third world. While there are many questionable fly-by-night fund-raising organizations out there, CNEC is not one of them. They have existed for forty years, they belong to both EFMA and IFMA, and they have learned how to make this kind of ministry work. Their philosophy is summed up in *Mission: A World-Family Affair* by Allen Finley and Lorry Lutz. Every year they channel about $2 million to worthwhile projects overseas.

Some missions specialize in the cultural mandate. They engage in projects which provide relief and development ministries to needy areas of the world. The World Relief Corporation is attached to the National Association of Evangelicals in the United States. Church World Service is a similar organization related to the National Council of Churches. Others are denominationally-oriented such as Mennonite Central Committee, while some are interdenominational like World Concern of Seattle, Washington. The giant of them all is World Vision International based in Monrovia, California, with an annual budget of over $100 million. Unlike some of the others, World Vision has a strong evangelistic component and each humanitarian project proposal must include an evangelistic impact report.

Where Does All the Money Come From?

The $1 billion plus that Americans spend yearly on missions comes almost entirely from voluntary contributions. Fortunately, the U.S. government, unlike those of many other nations, allows contributions to accredited missionary organizations to be deducted from taxable income. This increases incentive somewhat, but still most missions have to struggle to raise their operating funds.

Some do this quite successfully. Southern Baptists have the largest missionary budget in the country with an income of $109 million in 1981. Actually, World Vision International's is larger, but I am not including them here because some of their income comes from government sources rather than contributions from the Christian public. The other denominational missions with budgets in the tens of millions include Seventh-Day Adventists, Christian Churches/Churches of Christ, Assemblies of God, United Methodists, Church of the Nazarene, Christian & Missionary Alliance, and several more. Faith missions, generally speaking, run on lower budgets. The two largest are SIM International and TEAM.

Most missions spend most of their income in supporting field missionaries. The rule of thumb is to keep expenses of the home operation at less than 20 percent of the total budget, although some situations that involve fewer field missionaries will not permit this. Generally speaking, missions receive funds under one of two systems.

First, budgetary support. Large denominations which finance their own boards of missions often request their member churches to build into their local budgets annual grants to the board of missions of the denomination. In such cases, most funds are undesignated, and the people in the churches trust the mission board to allocate the funds competently. The missionaries themselves cooperate by keeping the churches informed as to what is happening on the field, but they do not have to be concerned with personal fund raising once they are accepted for missionary service.

Second, personalized support. All interdenominational missions, and many denominational missions such as Conservative Baptists and Assemblies of God, prefer the personalized system. Under this system, the missionary is responsible for raising personal support as well as additional funds for individual and mission projects on the field. This obviously puts pressure on the missionary, but it pays off in other ways. The donors, for example, are not giving just to "foreign missions" but to a particular missionary. They know the family personally. They pray for them regularly. They receive and read letters from the field. They watch the mission magazine for a word about the work of *their* missionary. Missionaries visit periodically on "deputation." To a much larger degree, the donors back home feel personally involved in the investment of their missionary dollars.

For many years it was not considered proper for missionaries to let other people know about their financial situation. They were only to pray, tell God of their needs, and trust God to lay the needs on the hearts of His people.

This silent, indirect approach is often traced to Hudson Taylor, who founded the China Inland Mission (now Overseas Missionary Fellowship) in 1865. In contemporary America, however, it is becoming passé, since most American donors prefer a more straightforward and businesslike approach. But the terminology has continued, and as a result missions that depend on personalized support are still widely known as "faith missions."

Dividing the Pie

Missions receiving budgetary support generally pay salaries and fringe benefits to the missionaries. They give them travel allowances, educational grants for their children, medical plans, and cost-of-living adjustments. The missionaries are treated much as a Shell Oil employee in a foreign country would be treated, except at a considerably lower salary.

Personalized support missions, however, cannot manage finances in the same way. Income will fluctuate depending on the success of workers in their fund-raising ministries. Since the individual missionaries are the ones who bring in the money, they naturally feel a little more concerned with how the pie is divided. Personalized support missions disburse their funds in one of two ways:

First, the individualized support system. Some missions, like Wycliffe Bible Translators and the New Tribes Mission, allow each missionary to have a large control over the funds they raise. All funds designated for support or work go directly to the missionary, less a deduction of something like 10 percent for home office expenses. After the worker subtracts an amount stipulated by the mission for family support, he or she in turn decides what aspect of the work the balance should be spent on. Sometimes a group of missionaries on a field will make joint decisions for the expenditure of some of their work funds. But all missionaries must spend these funds according to guidelines established by the U.S. Internal Revenue Service and keep close track of them. If they do not, the tax-exempt status of their mission is in jeopardy.

You can see that this system has the advantage of putting the money where the work is—out on the front lines. It also keeps pressure on the missionaries, for if their funds fall below the recommended support level, not only do they have nothing for their work but their salary is cut accordingly. Under this system some missionaries in the same mission handle much more money than others do.

Second, the pool system. In order to maintain more equity, some missions have developed the pool system. All funds raised by all missionaries (with the exception of designated work funds) go into the mission pool. Mission leadership then decides month by month how the pool is to be spent. One of the first items, of course, is salary, but every worker receives the same amount, occasionally with adjustments for size of family. The general director gets the same amount as the newly-arrived language school student. Decisions as to general expenses, or as to what project should be funded when, are made by the mission leadership, not by each individual. The theory behind this is that a community of Christians (the mission) can better discern the will of God for the work than can the individual.

How Missions Are Governed

The most common pattern of missionary government begins with a mission board of one kind or another here in the sending country. When the board is related to a denomination, the church's hierarchy usually selects its members in some way. When the board is an independent agency, it has a self-perpetuating board of directors, ordinarily chartered under the laws of one of the fifty states.

Some denominations, such as Conservative Baptists, allow their denominational board to function as an independent agency and gain considerable strength from such an arrangement.

The board usually appoints a chief administrative officer with a title such as general director or president who sets up an office in the U.S.A., meets regularly with the board, and runs the mission. He or she is assisted by a group of representatives at home who recruit missionaries and raise funds. On the other end they relate to the field director of each field and travel to visit the fields as much as possible. The final authority lies in the home board, however, and the degree of control of the home over the field varies greatly from mission to mission.

Some missions, however, have their board of directors on the field, with the board consisting mostly of field workers. The Overseas Missionary Fellowship is an example of a field-governed mission. Their general director is typically a field person, and they establish home *councils* (not boards) in the sending countries to handle mission affairs there. This pattern is most common with international missions, which employ missionaries from a variety of sending countries.

On the field, the workers usually gather in an annual field conference for spiritual nourishment and to transact mission business. The business agenda depends on the structure of the conference, but one almost universal item is the election of a field council and other officers.

Although there are infinite variations to these basic patterns, mission government is usually not complex. Responsible missions are very conscientious in keeping overhead down so that the maximum part of each dollar can be used on the field where the missionary work really is being done.

This is how the machinery runs. What specifically it

intends to accomplish we will discuss later. But right now, let's take a look at the responsibility of the home churches.

Do Something Now!

1. Write to five or six mission agencies of your choice. Ask them for information about their purpose, their ministries, their financial structure, their methods of raising funds, requirements for new workers, and current openings. When the replies come in, study them carefully and compare your findings. Try to include both denominational and faith missions on your list.

2. Borrow or purchase the current edition of *Mission Handbook: North American Protestant Ministries Overseas* edited by Samuel Wilson (MARC, 919 W. Huntington Drive, Monrovia, CA 91016). You would not read this from cover to cover any more than you would read a dictionary, but you should spend several hours handling it and becoming familiar with its contents so you can refer back to it whenever necessary.

Five
The Home Churches Behind the Missions

The word *missionary* comes from a Latin root that means "to send." Besides having what we called in chapter 3 the *missionary gift,* a true missionary is one who is *sent* to minister in another culture. This is why a British pastor, called to serve in an American church, is not considered a missionary as such. The pastor has been *called* by the church in America, not *sent* by the church or mission in England. Oh, the folks back home in the British church might say, "That's our missionary to America." But it is a popular, not a technical, use of the term. The church might have commissioned the pastor by laying on hands and praying God's blessing. But that is as far as it goes. Sending missionaries is quite a different thing.

This emphasis on sending comes out clearly in Romans

10, a passage we mentioned in chapter 2. There we stressed "How shall they hear without a preacher?" Here we will stress the important phrase, "How shall they preach unless they are *sent?*" (Rom. 10:15, italics added).

Missions usually begin in the home churches. The churches provide the personnel, the prayer, the funding, and the moral support. Paul's missionary band, as described in the New Testament, obviously received support from the churches. The book of Philippians is written much in the format of a modern missionary prayer letter including a word of thanks for past support and a gentle appeal for more (Phil. 4:10-19). If it weren't for the churches, there would be no missions.

Churches Nourish Missions

One of the emphases of the last chapter was that missions relate to churches as legs relate to the body. That chapter explained how the *legs* operate; this one will deal more with the *body's* role. The body nourishes and sustains the legs. The church nourishes and sustains the mission.

Obviously, missionaries are first of all members of churches. Although there are exceptions, the proper function of the church, as the Body of Christ, is to help each member find and use his or her spiritual gifts, and this of course includes the members with the missionary gift. Almost everyone who has been called to be a missionary can trace some of the roots of that call back to the local church. It is true that some discover their gift in a great missionary conference like the Inter-Varsity conference held every three years at Urbana, Illinois, or in a Bible study group, or at a Christian college, or perhaps while traveling abroad. But even in these cases, when the whole story is told, the home church has usually played an important part.

Thus the first major and essential contribution that home churches make to missions is to supply the personnel. Churches that build an adequate missionary emphasis into their regular teaching and program find that a steady stream of their people move out to the mission fields of the world. Not everybody in the church goes, of course. The whole body isn't an eye (1 Cor. 12:17), nor does everyone have the missionary gift. Year after year a good missionary-minded church may find from 1 to 5 percent of its members out on the mission fields at any given time. If your church has no missionary at all, this may say something about the health of your church in general.

The Blessing of Sending

Providing the missionaries, of course, is only the beginning. As the Bible says, they must be *sent*. Sending missionaries out is expensive, complicated, and time-consuming. But no part of the Christian life is more rewarding. An unwritten rule in the Kingdom of God is that the church that is doing its part in world missions is the church that God is blessing in every conceivable way.

One of the churches that supported me and my family throughout our missionary career came up against a severe financial crisis some years ago. The official board of the church called an emergency meeting, and all knew ahead of time that something unusual had to be done if the church was not to be shipwrecked financially. Soon after the meeting began, the pastor said, "Folks, I have been praying a good deal about our situation. I think the Lord has spoken to me about a solution. As a way out of our financial problem, would you consider raising our missionary budget?"

Some would have considered this a reckless and irresponsible proposal. Financially, it made no sense at all. But spiritually it did. And on the premise that God would take care of His Church if it continued faithful in spreading the gospel throughout the world, the deacons and trustees decided to step out on faith and try it. It worked! The entire church budget soon went into the black, and as far as I have heard has been there ever since. This is the kind of faith that God honors.

Once the church decides to do its part in the missionary task, it needs to adopt certain policies. These policies should be based on up-to-date knowledge of how missions operate and clear thinking on missionary strategy and the role of the church. A large amount of Christian good will goes down the drain each year because churches base their missionary programs on inadequate information, stick to outmoded policies, or otherwise squander their resources. Good will is not enough. One of the purposes of this chapter is to suggest some guidelines that will lead churches to establish sound and effective missionary policies.

"The Tin-Cup Complex"

A friend of mine, who served many years as a missionary and is now a pastor, recently wrote an article with the provocative title "Let's Banish Missionary Begging." He clearly sees both sides of the coin. He knows the viewpoints of both the mission and the church. He gives some sound advice. Surveys have shown that one of the most distasteful aspects of missionary service, particularly for young people today, is fund raising. I call it the "tin-cup complex."

Churches do well to reduce the tin-cup complex for missionaries as much as possible. It should not be the case, but it is painfully true that some young people today staunchly refuse missionary service not because they lack the gift but because they refuse to "rattle a tin cup." This is only one of the reasons why each church needs to make whatever adjustment is necessary in order to establish well-defined missionary financial policies.

Reducing the tin-cup complex does not mean that missionaries should no longer be dependent on churches. It may mean that in some cases the missionary will be more dependent. Dependence is a good thing. It keeps the home church praying and keeps the missionaries on their toes. Experience has shown that missionaries who go to the field financially independent have some disadvantages. At times their sense of commitment to the team is reduced, they are tempted to be disdainful of leadership, and their ties with the home church tend to become weakened. I myself can name some outstanding exceptions to this generalization, but they do not disprove the rule. A bond of dependence with the church strengthens missionary work and ultimately is a blessing to the church itself.

What I have said is not mere human calculation. A church missionary program must be based on biblical teaching, and the Bible is clear on this point. The key text is 2 Corinthians 8 and 9. There Paul is making an outright appeal for the Corinthians to contribute to a special offering he was taking for the poor in Jerusalem. They were asked to give even "beyond their ability," which is an exercise of faith, a spiritual dynamic which must not be overlooked. Churches which have taken bold steps of faith for missions testify that God has blessed them immeasurably.

How Much Missions Cost

How much does it cost to send a missionary family to the field these days? Like anything else, the cost rises with current inflationary trends. It is rising even faster in some parts of the world since the dollar has been devaluated on many foreign markets, decreasing the missionary's spending power there. One church recently had to add $17,000 to its annual missionary budget just to keep level with the official support increases of the mission boards. One thing this does *not* mean, however, is that missionaries are now getting rich!

Although Protestant missionaries do not take a formal vow of poverty as members of Catholic orders do, functionally it turns out that way for some. A large number of missionaries live their whole lives on subsistence income. Most are underpaid compared to others with similar training and experience in the United States. Some have retirement benefits and some do not. A few are paid at a level comparable to what they would receive pastoring a church in the U.S., but none would be classified as affluent unless they have some independent source of income.

When estimating the costs of sustaining a missionary program, such items as the following must be considered.

The missionaries' living expenses. A basic salary should include what is needed for food, clothing, housing, transportation, children's education, insurance, taxes, continuing education, vacation/recreation, and retirement. These are items which people back in the supporting churches need as well. In recent years the methods used by mission agencies to meet these needs have become very diverse. Some support the husband only, some give husband and wife equal salaries, some add on allowance for children and some do not. Some include housing and children's education in the salary, some give special additional allowances for that. Most mission agencies are more than willing to answer inquiries about their support systems.

Field ministry expenses. If you will look at most church budgets you will see that the salaries of the pastor and staff are only a portion of the whole. Substantial amounts are also budgeted for carrying on the ministry of the church. Likewise, mission programs require funds for carrying out the ministry once on the field. This is over and above salary. It does not make much sense to send missionaries and then fail to provide the tools they need to do a good job. Missionaries need regular discretionary funds for ongoing expenses. They also need funding for special projects which arise from time to time.

Outgoing and furlough expenses. One of the most expensive aspects of missionary funding is the transportation needed to get workers to and from the field. Outgoing expenses are steep, especially if the missionaries are going to a part of the world where they will need to take a substantial "outfit" along with them. Then the costs of returning to the home base on periodic furloughs should be planned from the start, along with what is necessary to return again to the field of service. While on furlough, transportation and often additional housing are needed. More and more workers are taking academic courses on furlough, and tuition needs to be provided. Continuing education in missiology is a good investment of time and money since missiological technology is improving so rapidly that few field missionaries can keep up. The increased efficiency on the field usually more than makes up for the cost.

Administrative expenses. The mission agency as well as the missionaries must be underwritten. Offices must be set up and equipment furnished. Executives need support as well as back-up staff such as secretaries and accountants. The typical travel budget for a mission executive is extremely high. Publicity and fund raising, including the publication of a mission magazine, need to be supported. Many mission agencies engage in valuable research and strategy development.

The costs of running a mission vary considerably. As I write I am looking at the current financial statements of four mission agencies. One spends 6 percent of the annual budget on administration, one 12 percent, one 15 percent, and one 25 percent. The percentage itself does not necessarily reflect the efficiency of the operation, since different agencies have different accounting methods for calculating these expenses.

The annual support package for a missionary family with two young children currently looks something like this in 1982 dollars:

Mission A (faith) $27,000
Mission B (denominational) 30,420
Mission C (denominational) 31,000
Mission D (faith) 33,540
Mission E (faith) 37,704

The important thing to remember is that whether we are talking about the astronomical total of $1 billion spent on missions annually in the U.S. or the more manageable $30,000 to support a missionary family, it all comes from church members.

What Is the Church's Part?

How much is a local church expected to do for missions?

Some churches have virtually no special interest in missions. As a matter of routine, they contribute to their denominational mission board program at the recommended level and let the board do the rest. Many of the members do not even know a real missionary personally, and their missionary I.Q. is practically zero. I have met Christian people like this and have found them usually very warm to missions. The fault generally is found not in the pew but in the pulpit. A missionary-minded pastor can do wonders for an entire church by developing a creative missionary program.

Some churches have decided to "tithe" their total income for missions. Ten percent of the annual budget goes for missions. This is often above denominationally recommended amounts, but it is far from outstanding. The rule of thumb for churches that have been fired with a vision for a lost world in need of Christ is one-third to one-half of the church budget for missions. Many spend at least as much on reaching others for Christ as they spend on their own needs.

Boston's historic Park Street Congregational Church has become a model for a successful missionary program. With an assist from another of missions' superchurches, People's Church in Toronto, they began their missionary effort in earnest in 1940. At that time church expenses were $31,000 and missionary giving totaled $17,000, which at 35 percent was not bad. But they reached the 50 percent mark in 1946, with over $50,000 for each item, hit a peak of 75 percent in 1957, and in 1972 they gave $364,593 to missions, a whopping 65 percent of the total budget. At this writing their annual missions giving has passed the $650,000 mark, still well over 50 percent of the church budget. Little wonder that God has blessed the church in other ways, and that for many years it was considered the number one evangelical church in New England.

Park Street Congregational, by the way, is not the only church over the half-million mark in missionary giving. The leader worldwide is Full Gospel Central Church in Seoul, Korea, which reports missionary contributions of $6 million per year. In North America Los Gatos Christian Church in Los Gatos, California gives $1.2 million to missions, and Peoples Church of Toronto, Canada is also over the $1 million mark. Grace Church of Edina, Minnesota is running over $800,000; Grace Community Church of the Valley in Panorama City, California, budgets $750,000; and my own church, Lake Avenue Congregational of Pasadena, California, is over $700,000. There are undoubtedly many more.

The Five Components of a Successful Program

Churches which have been most successful in building strong and effective missionary programs have usually given special attention to five components: building the committee, motivating the congregation, establishing the budget, raising the funds, and recruiting the missionaries. Let's look at them one at a time:

Building the committee. Back in 1973 God gave me a vision for something He wanted to do to help churches build a program for missions. I had been professionally involved in missions for many years before I realized how important chairpersons of local church missions committees are. A quick survey revealed that three Christian women, all of whom I knew personally, controlled over $1 million annually in mission funds. That was a large amount of money in those days—more than the annual income of 65 percent of the IFMA mission agencies. Those three women were chairpersons of their church's missions committees.

It dawned on me that those three women had incredible financial power. They themselves undoubtedly would never have associated their ministry with any sort of power at all. But I spent enough years as a mission executive to know that mission leaders hold such representatives of churches with large missionary budgets in great awe. I realized that if you were to add maybe 100 other missions chairpersons from comparable churches to these three, their combined wisdom could advance the missionary cause tremendously. I began to pray about the possibility of bringing those persons together in some kind of organization.

After discussing the matter with a number of colleagues, it became clear that the Lord was leading us to convene a National Institute for Missionary Committee Chairmen at the Fuller School of World Mission. This we did in June, 1974. Since this had never been done before, we had no idea of how much interest there might be in such an event. We were pleased when 128 persons showed up from fourteen states and nine denominations. The forty-eight-hour program was packed with speakers such as Donald McGavran, Arthur Glasser, Ted Engstrom, J. Edwin Orr, Charles Kraft, Vergil Gerber, and Ralph Winter, as well as missions committee chairpersons such as Katherine Coward of First Baptist Church, Van Nuys, California and Betty Vetterlein of Park Street Church, Boston, Massachusetts. Toward the end a suggestion was made to hold a business session, and the Association of Church Missions Committees (ACMC) was formed. Stephen Tavilla, missions chairperson of Grace Chapel, Lexington, Massachussetts was elected president of a board of directors, and Donald Hamilton, a lay leader of Bethany Church, Sierra Madre, California, and a person with extensive background in engineering and management, was named executive director.

Hamilton led the ACMC through seven years of substantial growth before stepping aside for his associate John C. Bennett to take over as executive director in 1981. Now based in Wheaton, Illinois, the ACMC has a membership list of over 500 churches from over thirty denominations. It operates on an annual budget of over $400,000. No longer must congregations grope around for help in building a strong missions committee. The expertise is now available. A key resource is the *Missions Policy Handbook,* a loose-leaf workbook which provides guidance for dealing with sixty different issues that need to be considered by churches and missions committees. One of the most valuable aspects of the ACMC program is an annual four-day national conference which draws together mostly lay members of local church missions committees who come to hear addresses by mission specialists and to learn how to make their missionary programs more effective. At this writing, attendance at the conferences is running 600-700. In the future ACMC leaders plan to hold the big conference in the Midwest every other year, and on alternate years schedule identical conferences on the east coast and on the west coast.

Crucial to building a strong missions committee is the choice of the leader. All too often church committees are chaired by persons selected on the basis of their good will and availability rather than because of their experience, expertise, and spiritual gifts. The missions committee should not be treated that way.

For one thing, the missions committee chairperson should become the missions expert of the church. We are now calling such persons "missions pros." Most good Christians are pro-missions, but few are missions pros. Some pastors feel they should be the missions pro of the church, and that is fine. But many pastors are delighted to have strong lay leaders running the mission program. And for this to happen, long terms of leadership are necessary. Churches which change their missions leaders every two or three years cannot hope for excellence. Even if a person is able to give considerable time to the job, it is hardly possible to become a missions pro in less than three to five years. And at that point the effectiveness is just beginning. Many churches which recognize this are adding ministers of missions to their staff on a full- or part-time basis. For some lay people, leadership in world missions can turn out to be a lifetime call.

Church missionary budgets need to include some items for local expenses. I believe that if a person is committed to leadership long-range, he or she ought to be asked to travel out to the mission fields on a regular basis. The itinerary ought to include visits to missionaries supported by the church as well as fact-finding trips to areas where God is at work in particularly dramatic ways. Additional travel funds are needed for domestic use such as ACMC conferences, both national and regional, workshops, and special study programs. A short time ago the missionary chairperson from Bel Air Presbyterian Church signed up for one of my seminary courses, just to be better informed.

Motivating the congregation. Even a national champion missions committee would not accomplish much if the congregation it represented were not turned-on for missions. How is this done? As in most aspects of church life, the inspiration must begin in the pulpit. If the pastor is excited about missions, if missions are frequently mentioned in the sermons, if world evangelization comes through loud and clear, if prayers go up for missionaries during the worship services, and if the pastor enthusiastically backs up the missions committee in every aspect of its work, a considerable start has been made toward motivating the congregation.

But even in churches fortunate enough to be pastored by a world Christian, special events are needed in order to highlight the blessings and challenges of world missions. One of the most immediate things to do is to start a Frontier Fellowship group in the church. This group meets once a month for prayer and discussion of missions. If your church is located in an urban area you can invite specialists from time to time to provide information and lead discussions. Each member of the group should have a copy of the *Daily Prayer Guide of the Frontier Fellowship* available from the U.S. Center for World Mission. Be sure the church library is well stocked with books on missions. Some of them can be read and used as a basis for Frontier Fellowship discussions.

An annual missionary conference is a tried and true method of motivating Christian people for missions. There are many variations of format for missionary conferences, but the total impact should be to inform the congregation about what is happening in missions around the world, to update them on the works and workers supported by the church, and to challenge them for expanded service and giving.

The missionary conference has been the cornerstone of the development of Park Street Church's outstanding missionary program in Boston. It begins on a Friday in the spring, and runs through the week to the following Sunday. Mission societies strive to send their best representatives to the conference, and it is considered a great privilege to be invited to speak. Each agency sets up attractive displays, designed to give the people an opportunity to see firsthand some of the things the missions are doing, and to pick up the latest literature. Missionaries themselves are housed in the homes of church families so the people and the missionaries can get to know each other firsthand. This conference is so well planned that some people who do not live in the Boston area take a week's vacation, stay in a hotel, and benefit greatly from the conference.

Establishing the budget. In order to maintain maximum challenge, the missionary committee should have the responsibility of designing the budget and of raising and spending the funds. Major items for a missionary budget will include:

1. Overhead. The costs of running the church missionary program are sometimes met from general funds and sometimes from funds designed from missions income. In any case, they should show in the total missions budget.

2. Contribution to the denominational program. This naturally applies only to denominational churches. The amount of contribution depends on a multitude of variable factors, one of which is the degree to which the

local church feels a part of the total program. For some churches such as Christian and Missionary Alliance and Southern Baptist, this item might include nearly all the missionary giving of the congregation.

3. Direct support of missionaries. For many churches, this is the largest item in the budget. Some churches give small amounts to a great many missionaries, some give substantial amounts (up to full support) to a limited number of missionaries. While there are arguments on both sides, in my view it is not helpful to spread missionary funds too thinly. Some are suggesting that churches strive for 60 percent to 100 percent support to missionaries who come from within their own ranks, and not drop below $200 per month of support for others. The ACMC says, "Your church should seek to take the burden of financial worry off your missionaries." In that way the churches will at least be assured that their own missionaries spend a reasonable part of their furlough in the local community, to the mutual benefit of the church and the missionary family alike.

Funds are needed not only for the regular support of missionaries but also for special needs. The printing and mailing of prayer letters, for example, is one item often overlooked by the church—only to become a great source of concern to the missionary. It is well to keep aside some contingency funds for emergency needs of the more heavily supported workers.

4. Project support. A portion of each year's budget should be available for the funding of projects that come to the attention of the missionary committee. Many of these projects will be related to the work that the church's own missionaries are doing, but some will not. Again, contingency funds are helpful in this category.

5. Research. For much too long the value of

research for the missionary enterprise has been under-estimated. Many of the great advances in world evangelization today can be attributed to the acceleration of missiological research over the past couple of decades, but what has been done is only a start. Some church missions budgets now include scholarships for graduate study and support funds for the major missiological research centers. Dean Paul Pierson of the Fuller Seminary School of World Mission says, "I believe that one of the most strategic investments that a church missions committee can make is to designate at least 5 percent of the annual missionary budget for missiological research."

6. Continuing education for missionaries. This has already been mentioned under missionary furlough costs, but it bears repeating. Effectiveness in missionary work can be increased dramatically if the workers can plug into the new technology available to them. Missiology is an extremely rapidly developing field, and some catch-up study should be built into every furlough. And the funds for this should be provided by the missionary budgets of the supporting churches.

Raising the funds. In order to raise the funds necessary for a well-rounded missionary budget, churches usually adopt (with certain variations) one of three plans:

First, the church budget plan. Under this plan, the missionary budget becomes a part of the total church budget. It is presented along with Christian education, staff salaries, building maintenance, music ministry, evangelism, and whatever else the church does. This has some advantages. For one thing, a general financial appeal is made to the congregation only once a year. For another, it can truly be said that every dollar you give to the church budget includes x number of cents for missions. All church giving, to a certain extent, is

missions giving. While this fits well into some churches'
philosophies of ministry, others take a different route.

Second, the single offering plan. Southern Baptists
have developed the single offering plan to a science.
Every Southern Baptist congregation takes up a special
Christmas offering called the Lottie Moon Offering. It is
named after a Southern Baptist missionary to China
who made the initial suggestion for such an offering in
1887. A great deal of excitement is generated around
this offering throughout the nation, and not a little com-
petition between pastors tends to build up. When a pastor is nominated for a denominational position, for
example, a large Lottie Moon offering usually attracts
votes in the convention. The goal of Christmas 1982
was $58 million. If recent trends hold true they should
be able to meet their 1983 goal of $66 million in the one
offering.

Third, the faith-promise system. In recent years
more and more churches have been switching to the
faith-promise system. One of the reasons is that it
seems to work so well. Another is that the Association
of Church Missions Committees actively endorses it.
The ACMC says, "To stimulate and direct increased
giving to world missions, set your missions budget
apart from the rest of your church's budget and under-
write it through faith promise." In the annual missionary
conference each member or family is challenged to pray
and seek God's will for how much they should give to
missions in excess of their regular church pledge. Most
are encouraged to have faith that this money will come
in over and above what they anticipate as normal family
income over the next year. I have heard numerous tes-
timonies of the fun people have had in watching God
bring in those funds from unanticipated and often
unusual sources.

This actually happened in a church that we belonged to for some years. A few years ago, when the missions budget of $7,200 was simply a part of the regular church budget, the whole church as well as the building fund went into the red. Finances became critical, so the missionary committee suggested switching over to the faith-promise system for missions, mainly in order to relieve the general church budget. For that first year no specific goal was stated, but during the year all the $7,200 came in *apart from regular church giving*. The church itself went into the black and now has burned the mortgage!

The following year, they still were "ye of little faith" and set only $7,200 as the new goal. However, missionary giving went up to $8,500, and for the first time the committee had a surplus. In the third year, the goal was $11,640, and the fourth was $15,000. Doubling missionary giving in four years and adding to the general church budget at the same time constitute a good record in anyone's book. But for those who take the faith-promise system seriously, it seems to be the rule, not the exception.

Take Grace Evangelical Church of College Park, Georgia as another example. It is a new church with an attendance of about 200 which still meets in a public school. Pastor Bill Waldrop is a world Christian. In order to expand his vision he attended the ACMC annual conference in 1976. He discovered the importance of strong lay leadership for missions and appointed Mary Lou Bohnsack as missions coordinator for the church. He heard about the faith-promise system for missions giving and immediately challenged the congregation with it. The first faith promise was $5,000, but the second year it jumped to $35,000. Now the church gives 50 percent of its total income or over

$100,000 to missions. Among other things, it supports twenty-one foreign missionaries and six home missionaries. Pastor Bill says, "Despite all opposition, the Lord will bless you because the world of lost people is on His heart."

Do Something Now!

1. Send $3.50 to the Association of Church Missions Committees, P.O. Box ACMC, Wheaton, Illinois 60187. Request a pack of five "Self-Evaluation Profiles." When they arrive, have five knowledgeable persons in your church fill them out independently, and then compare the results.

2. When you write, also ask the ACMC for information concerning membership. Take the materials to your pastor or missions chairperson so they can consider membership in case your church does not already belong.

3. Read *The Senders: World Missions Conferences and Faith Promise Offerings* by Paul B. Smith (G. R. Welch Co., Ltd., Toronto, Canada). Paul Smith, pastor of Peoples Church in Toronto, Canada, operates what has been regarded through the years as one of the premier missions conferences. Peoples Church, as far as I know, was the first to see a missions budget of over $1 million.

4. If you really want depth, order the *Missions Policy Handbook* from ACMC and work your way through it either by yourself or with a discussion group.

Six
The Fourth Dimension of Missions: Strategy

Fourth dimensions are not always the most obvious. For many years philosophers and physicists alike described the world as three-dimensional having height, breadth, and depth. Then along came Einstein, and since then that elusive factor of time has been recognized as the fourth dimension.

Missions have a similar story. The first three dimensions are much more prominent in sermons, hymns, and textbooks than the fourth. The first dimension of missions is *height*—the relationship of people to God, reconciliation, the new birth. The second dimension is *depth*—personal holiness, spirituality, being "endued with power from on high" (Luke 24:49). The third dimension is *breadth*—witnessing, sharing Christ with those who are not yet Christians.

All three dimensions are essential to missions. But there is a fourth equally essential—*strategy*. Because strategy often tends toward the pragmatic, it appears to some as not being spiritual, and I have come up against some staunch resistance to developing it in any detail. An increasing number of missiologists, however, are recognizing the obvious fact that the use of the human mind is not always antagonistic to the Holy Spirit. After all, Jesus told us to love God with all our heart, with all our soul, and *with all our mind* (Matt. 22:37). This is why I don't feel bad at all about using my mind as much as possible in developing missionary strategy. Of course, in order to avoid the dangers of carnality, the height and depth dimensions described above must be properly cared for as indispensable preconditions. I want to develop this spiritual dimension in more detail in the next chapter.

Strategy Is Not Optional

When you think of it, if you take Jesus and His Lordship at all seriously you are forced to develop a strategy of some kind. He demands that His stewards be found faithful (1 Cor. 4:1-2). Faithfulness, pure and simple, is doing what your Master tells you to do and accomplishing the goals He sets for you. The parable in Matthew 25:14-30, known as the Parable of the Talents, is a parable about stewards. Two of the three used good strategy and accomplished their master's goals (in that case, making wise investments of capital) and were called "good and *faithful* servant." One did not, and he was called "wicked and lazy." Anyone who does not take strategy seriously runs the risk of missing the reward at the judgment.

Strategy is simply the means agreed upon to reach a certain goal. Missionary strategy is the way the Body of Christ goes about obeying the Lord and accomplishing the objectives He lays down. Every Christian every day uses strategy of some kind or other in the attempt to do God's will. However, it is clear that some strategies are demonstrably superior to others. It is up to each one of us to examine the options and choose the best.

The best strategy is, first of all, *biblical* because God's work must be done in God's way. Second, it is *efficient*. Since our personnel, money, and time are all limited, we need to make decisions sooner or later as to what priorities to assign in their use. We can't do everything we would like to do, so we must decide what to do and what to leave undone. We should make this decision largely on the basis of efficiency—do what will best accomplish God's objective, so long as the methods are pleasing to God as well. Third, strategy must be *relevant*. Missions is such a fast-moving field that strategy useful five years ago might well be obsolete today. It needs constant updating.

The Four Strategies of Missions

Modern missionary strategy must not be regarded in a simplistic manner. For maximum effectiveness in world evangelization, many components must fit together properly. In order to understand what the principal components are, I like to think of them under four strategies of mission. I will list them here for convenience and then discuss each one in detail.

Strategy I—the right goals

Stragegy II—the right place at the right time

Strategy III—the right methods

Strategy IV—the right messengers.

Strategy I—the Right Goals

Every one of Jesus' commands to His people contains a goal of some kind. There are hundreds of them in the New Testament, and faithful servants will want to obey them all in every way possible. But one command above all others contains the goal for missions, and against that goal we must evaluate all missionary strategy. This commandment is known as the "Great Commission" and is found in Matthew, Mark, Luke, John, and Acts.

A proper understanding of the Great Commission will give us a clear picture of what God's goals for missions are. It goes without saying that God's goals are the *right goals*.

The place to start is Matthew 28:19-20, the most detailed and complete summary of the Great Commission. A proper interpretation of these verses will provide us with the key needed to understand the others in context. Here is what the text says: "Go therefore and make disciples of all nations, baptizing them in the name of the Father and of the Son and of the Holy Spirit, teaching them to observe all things that I have commanded you."

Notice that the passage contains four action verbs: *go, make disciples, baptize,* and *teach.* In the original Greek only one of them is imperative and three are participles. The imperative *make disciples* is the heart of the command. The participles *going, baptizing,* and *teaching* are helping verbs.

Making disciples, then, is the end. It is the *right goal* of mission strategy. Going, baptizing, and teaching are means to be used toward accomplishing the end. They are also necessary components of missionary strategy, but they are not ends in themselves.

The other four appearances of the great commission do not expand on the right goal. They do add to the list of the means available to reach it. Mark 16:15-16 repeats baptizing but adds preaching. Luke 24:47-48 repeats preaching but adds witnessing. John 20:21 mentions sending. Acts 1:8, also written by Luke, repeats witnessing and adds the geographical aspect of Jerusalem, Judea, Samaria, and the uttermost part of the earth.

Now I will make a rather bold statement. *In my judgment, the greatest error in contemporary missionary strategy is the confusion of means and end in the understanding of the Great Commission.*

In other words, some missions and missionaries have set up their programs as though some of the means were ends in themselves. They have not adequately articulated what they are doing in terms of making disciples. Some, for example, have contented themselves with preaching the gospel whether or not their preaching makes disciples. Some have very meticulously counted "decisions," but they make no corresponding effort to count and report *disciples.* This is why some evangelistic reporting seems inflated. Just to know how many attended an evangelistic crusade or even how many signed decision cards is helpful, but inadequate. The Lord of the Great Commission, in the final analysis, is interested in *disciples,* not simply *decisions.*

Don't forget, when we talk about right goals we are talking about goals for the whole Body of Christ, not just for individuals. As we have seen, the doctrine of spiritual gifts teaches us that we all make different contributions. But as all members of the Body work together, the final result should be new disciples. Success or failure must be measured ultimately in those terms. One entire mission might concentrate on translating the Bible, for example. Bible translation is an essential function of the Body, for without the Word of God in the language of each people they will not be able to hear the message of salvation. But proper strategy will coordinate this work with that of other members of the Body so that translated Bibles become not just some rather exotic contributions to the literature of humankind but effective instruments for making disciples. In other words, Bible translation or radio broadcasting or door-to-door visitation are not ends in themselves. They are means toward making disciples.

At this point be careful of the definition of *disciple*. If the right goal of missionary strategy is to make *disciples,* you have to know what Jesus was talking about if you plan to obey Him. You have to know how you can tell when you have made one. Nebulous ideas of what disciples are only serve to blur good strategy.

People are not disciples just because they have been born in a Christian country or, in many cases, even if they are church members. We have already mentioned that decisions in themselves do not necessarily lead to disciples. Not everyone who prays to receive Jesus ends up a disciple. The basic meaning of disciple in the New Testament is equivalent to a true, born-again Christian.

In order to make a disciple you need to go to the fourth world, to people not yet true Christians. Unsaved people are the raw material, so to speak, for fulfilling the Great Commission. The instant one becomes a new creation in Christ (2 Cor. 5:17), you have made a disciple.

Some have confused "making disciples" with "discipleship." *Making disciples* is the right goal of evangelism and missions according to the Great Commission. Once disciples are made, they then begin the lifetime road of *discipleship.* Helping people along the road is another important Christian ministry, an essential function of the Body, but one step past the goal of the Great Commission. Even the participle "teaching" in the Great Commission itself does not refer to the details of the road of discipleship, as some might think. The thing Jesus wants us to teach at that point in time is "to observe," not "all things I have commanded you." Part of becoming a disciple is to be disposed to obey Jesus as Lord. The details come later as the new disciple travels down the road of discipleship in the stage of Christian development that Donald McGavran calls "perfecting."

What does a disciple look like? How can you tell one when you see it? Acts 2 gives us a helpful indication. On the day of Pentecost three thousand disciples were made. The reason we know they were disciples and not just people who made "decisions" is that when Luke looked back in preparation for writing the book of Acts, they "continued steadfastly in the apostles' doctrine and fellowship, in the breaking of bread, and in prayers" (Acts 2:42). Outsiders can recognize disciples because they "have love for one another" (John 13:35). In clearer terms, a disciple is a responsible church member.

If a mission society moves into a pagan village one year, and moves out three years later leaving a group of 250 people who declare that Christ is their Lord, who meet together regularly for worship, who read the Bible and pray—they have made 250 disciples and to that degree have fulfilled the Great Commission. Now, these disciples might lack a great deal of polish. Many yet may be babes in Christ. They might not act like Wheaton, Illinois Christians. They might have a long way to go down the road of Christian discipleship, but nevertheless they are disciples. If the mission in question reports its results in such terms, it has properly understood Strategy I. It is aiming for the *right goals*.

Strategy II—the Right Place at the Right Time

Strategy II is best understood in agricultural terms. It comes out most clearly in some of Jesus' rural-oriented parables. As a farmer myself (my college degree is in dairy production!), I often jestingly suggest that being a farmer is sometimes more helpful in interpreting the parables than knowing Greek! The helpful aspect is that every farmer, by nature, has what I call the *vision of the fruit.*

No farmer works fields for the fun of it—he or she works for the payoff, which is the fruit. A person buys a farm on the anticipation that it will produce fruit. A farmer may enjoy mechanics, but working on the machinery is not an end in itself. It eventually helps get the fruit. Farmers sow seed and cultivate crops not because they think it's fun to ride tractors but because, if they don't, there will be no fruit. "He who sows and he who reaps may rejoice together" (John 4:36). Why? Because they gather fruit together.

Sound missionary strategy never loses the vision of the fruit. Strategy I teaches us that in missionary work this fruit is *disciples*. Keep this vision foremost in sowing, pruning, and reaping.

The vision for sowing. The Parable of the Sower appears in Matthew, Mark, and Luke. The briefest summary is in Luke 8:4-15. It tells of a farmer who sowed seeds on four different parts of his farm, but got fruit on only one. Anyone with the vision of the fruit will instantly ask, "Why?" Jesus' disciples undoubtedly asked the same thing when they first heard it.

According to Jesus' interpretation, the variable factor was not the sower, nor was it the seed (which is described as the "word of God"), nor was it the method. It was the soil. No matter how good the seed is, any farmer knows it will not bear fruit on roadways, on rocky soil, or among thorns. In order to produce fruit, good seed must be sown in fertile soil.

The obvious lesson for missionary strategy is that the seed of the Word must be concentrated on fertile soil if fruit is to be expected. Some peoples of the world are receptive to the gospel while others are resistant. The world's soils should be tested before sowing the seed. Concentrating, come what may, on rocky soil, whether or not any disciples are made, is foolish strategy. Farmers who have the vision of the fruit do not make that mistake too often, but some missiologists unfortunately do. This is the "right place" aspect of Strategy II.

The vision for pruning. The Parable of the Fig Tree in Luke 13:6-9 is seen as a threat by some missionaries. If they are guided by the vision of the fruit, however, it should not be.

The farmer who came along and saw a beautiful fig tree was forced to look a little closer. The problem there was comparable to many mission fields. The fig tree itself had grown well, but there were no figs! Much missionary "work" has likewise developed to a high degree, but there is little or no fruit—no disciples are being made. The farmer in the parable is a good strategist. When there is no fruit after much work and a prudent time lapses, he says cut it down—change your program. He operates on the basis of the vision of the fruit. His hired man does not share the vision because the hired man's income depends not so much on harvest as on a salary. His strategy is to continue the work as long as he can. The hired man, like many missionaries, is program-centered, not goal-centered.

Missionaries who are comfortably settled into a certain "program" or "missionary work" would do well to examine what they are doing in terms of the vision of the fruit. It is not easy to change a program, especially when you have been hoping against hope that in a year or so it will begin bearing fruit. But too often these years have stretched out into lifetimes. Missionaries who could have spent ten years making disciples spend the same ten years simply doing "missionary work" because they lack the courage to cut the barren fig tree down and change their program.

The vision for reaping. When Jesus talks to His disciples about reaping, for the first time He mentions the need for praying that the Lord of the harvest will "send out laborers into His harvest" (Matt. 9:37-38). When the "laborers are few" the farmer runs the risk of losing some of the harvest. The Strategy II aspect in this case is the *right time*. Laborers are not needed when the harvest is still green, nor are they needed when the harvest has passed. Timing is of utmost importance in any harvest.

Suppose, for example, that you owned an apple orchard. In Field *A* a worker would harvest five bushels in an hour. In Field *B* it would take five hours to harvest just one bushel. In Field *C* nothing could be harvested because the apples are all still green. If you had thirty workers today, where would you send them? I think I would send twenty-nine of them to Field *A* so as not to lose the fruit there. I would send the other one to do what could be done in Field *B* and also to keep an eye on Field *C*. The job would be to let me know when those fields were ripe so I could redeploy the personnel.

Parallel situations arise time after time in missionary work. Some peoples are ready to be harvested today, some are not yet ready. These "unresponsive peoples" should not be neglected—someone should be there who is expert enough to tell when they are becoming ripe for the gospel. In one sense you need the very finest workers in the unresponsive fields. But no one who takes strategy seriously would advocate a massive labor force in green fields. Jesus wouldn't. He does not tell us to pray for more laborers to go to green fields or to fallow fields. The laborers are needed for the *ripe harvest fields*.

Right after Jesus says that (Matt. 9), He sends His own harvesters out (Matt. 10). There were three fields in those days: Jews, Gentiles, and Samaritans. Only the Jews were ripe at the time. Jesus specifically tells His disciples not to go to the Gentiles and Samaritans (Matt. 10:5—the green fields), but to go to the Jews (Matt. 10:6). Later on, both the Gentiles and the Samaritans ripened and bore much fruit, but not at that time.

The People Approach to World Evangelization

Exactly how to go about discerning the fields and making plans for sowing the seed or reaping the harvest is one of the key issues of mission strategy. As I mentioned in the first chapter, the feeling among many missiologists is that over the past decade or so the most significant change in thinking about missionary strategy is what the Lausanne Committee for World Evangelization (LCWE) has labeled "the people approach to world evangelization."

The basic idea behind this is that human beings are not simply unrelated individuals. Each person is identified with a social group that becomes a very important part of his or her self-identity. That social group is called a "people" and is defined technically as "a significantly large sociological grouping of individuals who perceive themselves to have a common affinity for one another. For evangelistic purposes it is the largest group within which the gospel can spread without encountering barriers of acceptance or understanding." Each one of these people groups must be evangelized on its own terms. The notion can be traced back to the homogenous unit principle of church growth taught by noted missiologist Donald McGavran. Its importance is one of the factors which prompts Professor Herbert Kane of Trinity Evangelical Divinity School to describe church growth as "the most dynamic movement in mission circles in recent years."

Just how the people approach works into practical missions strategy planning has been developed chiefly by a consortium of research agencies centered in Pasadena, California, including the Fuller Seminary School of World Mission, the MARC division of World Vision International, and the U.S. Center for World Mission. Their activities have been coordinated by the LCWE Strategy Working Group which was chaired successively by myself (of Fuller) and Edward Dayton (of World Vision). One of the major results is a series of annual reports called *Unreached Peoples,* which began in 1979. As of this writing, over three thousand unreached people groups have been identified and described.

Among other things, the U.S. Center has been concentrating on describing the total task remaining. Their full color chart, designed by Ralph Winter and Bruce Graham and called "Unreached Peoples of the World-1983," lays it out beautifully. The challenge is summarized succinctly in these words: "The areas indicated on the chart below correspond to the number of individuals making up the 'hidden,' 'unreached,' or 'frontier' peoples of the world—those groups that still have no church or (usually) any significant mission work reaching out to them. These large blocks of people speak over 5,000 mutually unintelligible languages, and are further broken down into approximately 16,750 nations/peoples, each of which requires specialized cross-cultural outreach and its own indigenous church."

Once people groups are identified, the Strategy II principle of the right time and the right place can then be applied. An example of this is given by Edward Pentecost of Dallas Seminary in his book *Issues in Missiology.* Pentecost tells of the Maguzawa people of Nigeria, an animistic tribe which had rejected the Islamic rule and religion centuries ago. The Maguzawa were not particularly inclined to hear the Christian gospel any more than they were the teaching of Islam until quite recently. Apparently the harvest had not yet ripened. But then the Nigerian government began to require elementary school for all its citizens, and religious training was a required part of the curriculum. Parents had a right to choose whether their children would study the Koran or the Bible. When the crunch came, their hatred for Islam was stronger than their indifference toward Christianity, so almost all the

Maguzawa parents chose the Bible for the children to study.

A tremendous change began to take place. Pentecost, applying Strategy II, says, "The Evangelical Church of West Africa has found itself with a ripe harvest field into which it is sending its field evangelists to reap the harvest while it is ripe." What has happened? "Today there is a turning to Christ that is so fast that the church cannot keep up with the baptism of new believers." Pentecost himself recently spent several months among the Maguzawa to help set up a crash program of ministerial training. He is well tuned to modern missiological strategy.

Strategy III—the Right Methods

When there is much work and little or no fruit, something is wrong. Careful analysis will usually pinpoint the trouble as either working in unripe fields or working in ripe fields but using wrong methods. You can go into a perfectly ripe field of wheat and work your head off, but if you are using a cornpicker you will get nothing. Potato diggers are useless in apple orchards.

Around the world there are some people groups who would gladly receive the gospel and become Jesus' disciples, but missionaries among these people are not making disciples because they are using inappropriate methods.

The wrong language is one of the common methodological mistakes. In many cases on record the missionary thought that preaching in the trade language would be adequate for making disciples. Only through switching to the local dialect, the language of the heart, however, did the fruit begin to come. If the missionary had refused to change methods, no amount of hard work would have done the job.

Forcing individuals from different people groups to mix in primary group relationships has often proved to be another wrong method. For many years, for example, the Oregon Friends were reaping a great harvest among the Aymaras of Bolivia, while others working equally as hard were not. It was then discovered that the Friends insisted on keeping their churches purely Aymara, while others thought it better to mix *mestizo* believers with Aymaras. This is another application of the homogeneous unit principle of church growth. Churches of one kind of people only are usually more effective in winning others of the same people. In Bolivia the method again made the difference.

An unusual example of how changing the method made a great deal of difference comes from George Samuel of India. It began at the Lausanne Congress of 1974 when Samuel read the *Unreached Peoples Directory* prepared for the Congress by Edward Dayton of MARC. Samuel discovered that in his area of Kerela was a group of people called Cholanaikkans. He had never heard of them, but God gave him a strong burden of prayer for them. When he returned to India he began to make inquiries. He learned that the Cholanaikkans were a tribe of naked, fair-skinned people who lived in caves in the Mangeri Hills. They ate fruit, plants, and wild honey. They had never learned how to cook. They did not bathe, cut their hair, shave, or clean their teeth. They wrapped themselves in the bark of trees when it got cold. They had never heard the gospel of the love of Jesus Christ.

George Samuel gathered some of his Christian friends to join in prayer, and soon they formed a new mission agency called Tribal Missions. Their first target was the Cholanaikkans. They soon discovered that the tribe was not easy to locate. They lived deep in the hills, and the only way there was to go through the forests on foot. On their first attempt they met swarms of dangerous mosquitoes which caused fever and they had to turn back. On the second trip they got past the mosquitoes but were terrified by wild elephants. However, they found the Cholanaikkans that time. When the naked Cholanaikkans spotted the missionaries approaching they fled into their caves, and the friendly noises the missionaries were trying to make did not seem to coax them out.

Here is where Strategy III comes in. Whatever method they were using had not worked to that point. Something different was needed. Then it occurred to the Christians what needed to be done. They took off their shirts and trousers, leaving just a minimum of cloth around their waists. When they approached again, practically naked themselves, some of the braver men came out of their caves. Through repeated visits, the missionaries gained their confidence and began ministering to their physical needs. Soon they were able to share the gospel, and three years later over half the Cholanaikkans had become baptized believers, disciples of Jesus Christ. Not only that, but through this contact, the missionaries have discovered three more neighboring unreached people groups.

Methods must be selected on largely pragmatic considerations since the Bible does not pretend to give twentieth-century instructions. Therefore, it is good strategy not only to set measurable goals but also to build in from the start of the effort instruments for measuring its success or failure. Only by doing this will it be possible to look back and know which methods God has blessed and which methods He has not blessed. One of the most curious facts in modern missions is that this simple procedure is so seldom carried out.

Let me take a final illustration of Strategy III from the extremely important ministry of Bible translation.

One of the most innovative and aggressive new Bible translation ventures is Living Bibles International (LBI). Founded in 1968 by Kenneth N. Taylor, translator of *The*

Living Bible, LBI is currently working in the 110 major languages of the world. The intention of this massive multi-million dollar program is to produce Scriptures in simple, readable and understandable language. The translations are not word-for-word, but thought-for-thought. This methodology, called dynamic equivalence by professionals, produces a Bible which the common people are greatly attracted to. In English, for example, *The Living Bible's* sales have gone over the twenty-six million mark. Choosing this philosophy of translation is one outstanding application of Strategy III.

But translating the Scriptures is only the first step. The second is to get them into the hands and minds of the people. In order to make this happen, LBI uses creative methodologies. For instance, in Catholic Poland, the Jesus film, produced and distributed by Campus Crusade, is currently being shown to twenty million Poles over a three-year period. On the average, 10 percent of those who see the film make a decision to commit their lives to Jesus Christ. The sound track of the Jesus film uses only the text of the Gospel of Luke. What could be more appropriate to give to their inquirers than a Gospel of Luke? LBI has picked up this challenge and is in the process of distributing five million copies of the Polish living Luke with the imprimatur of the Catholic hierarchy. By the same token, in Italy LBI has arranged to have their living New Testament, including the four spiritual laws of Campus Crusade, printed by none other than the Vatican Press. Traditional methodologies of Bible distribution obviously have been improved by LBI.

Strategy IV—the Right Messengers

Some things God does by Himself; some things He does by using human beings.

It seems, for example, that the difference between

fertile and barren soil is basically a matter of divine providence. The ripening of certain harvest fields at certain times can be attributed only to the sovereignty of God. "I planted, Apollos watered," writes Paul, "but *God gave the increase*" (1 Cor. 3:6, italics added).

God brings the harvest to ripeness but He does not harvest it. He uses Christian people to accomplish that task, and He is glorified when His people "bear much fruit" (John 15:8). He is particularly interested "that your fruit should remain" (John 15:16). But how does this fruit come? The servant of God can bear fruit only if the branch abides in the vine. Jesus is the vine, and Christian people are the branches.

Strategy IV, then, stresses the right messengers. The right messengers are people filled with the Holy Spirit. They abide in Jesus. They are fully committed. They take up their cross daily and follow their Master. Without Strategy IV, the first three strategies are dead letters. That is why Jesus insisted that His disciples not begin their missionary work until they were "endued with power from on high" (Luke 24:49).

I want to elaborate on this concept of power in the next chapter.

Do Something Now!

1. If you did not send in your $1.00 to the U.S. Center for World Mission (1605 Elizabeth Street, Pasadena, California 91104) requesting their chart "Unreached Peoples of the World-1983" as I suggested in chapter 1, do it now. It should be clear that some of the most crucial information for mission strategy is to understand the unfinished task in terms of unreached or frontier peoples.

2. Read either one of these two books:

That Everyone May Hear by Edward R. Dayton (MARC, 919 W. Huntington Drive, Monrovia, California

91016). This is a simple and inexpensive summary of the strategy planning system used by the LCWE Strategy Working Group.

Planning Strategies for World Evangelization by Edward R. Dayton and David A. Fraser (Wm. B. Eerdmans Publishing Co.). This book expands the above into 530 pages, and is an indispensable guide if you are going to undertake serious planning for mission strategy.

3. Order from MARC (919 W. Huntington Drive, Monrovia, California 91016) one or more of the *Unreached Peoples* annuals and become familiar with the kind of information that is available on unreached peoples. If you also use the Frontier Fellowship's *Daily Prayer Guide,* you will have a constant inflow of new information on unreached peoples. You get the Prayer Guide free when you order the chart "Unreached Peoples of the World—1983."

Seven

The Power Source for Missions

In the last chapter I pointed out that all the carefully planned missionary strategy in the world will be of no avail unless it is activated by divine power. According to our records, the very last words Jesus spoke to His disciples before He left this earth were: "You shall receive power when the Holy Spirit comes upon you; and you shall be witnesses for Me in Jerusalem, and in all Judea and Samaria, and to the end of the earth" (Acts 1:8). Knowing that they could not be effective in their future ministry without power, the disciples went back to Jerusalem and "all continued with one accord in prayer and supplicaton" (Acts 1:14).

Power Begins with Prayer
Prayer has been preached, taught, sung about, and

generally extolled in every church I have been connected with. But as I think back I cannot recall that it has been practiced to any particularly great degree. Meetings called specifically for prayer are usually not the best attended. Certain individuals, particularly those with a gift of intercession, are there at the meetings and a few others as well, but often the excitement level is relatively low compared to other activities of the church. Every American Christian leader I know feels that we are underprayed. The Bible seems to describe the prayer dimension of the Christian life-style in terms that most of us do not seem to reflect. Knowing this, most pastors, and rightly so, admonish their congregations to take prayer more seriously. But it frequently stops there. How can we make it actually happen?

When I go to Korea I see quite a different role of prayer in ordinary Christian living. Every morning at 4:30 or 5:00 a prayer meeting is held in every church. This includes rural and urban churches, large and small churches, and churches of all denominations. The prayer meeting convenes 365 mornings a year. When I first began to observe this phenomenon I simply assumed that in a large, multiple staff church the associate pastors or trained lay leaders would conduct the dawn prayer meeting, as it is called, while the senior pastor stayed in bed for much-needed rest. But I soon found out that this was not so. Most senior pastors themselves conduct the dawn prayer meeting personally. I have asked several of them why they do this. Their answers are typically short and direct: "Because that's where the power is!" They are convinced that their spirits can no more function well without a daily intake of prayer power than their bodies can without daily intake of food.

A large number of the Korean churches, perhaps the majority, also have an all-night prayer meeting every Friday night. Some add another on Wednesday nights. And these church activities are over and above the personal devotional time practiced diligently by believers.

My good friend Kim Sundo, who pastors the ten-thousand-member Kwang Lim Methodist Church in Seoul, has a literal prayer closet built into his pastor's study. It has a mat on the floor, a little stand which holds a Bible, and a picture of Jesus on the wall. He told me, quite casually, that he spends an hour and a half per day in the prayer closet. Also connected to the study is a bedroom with a full bath. Kim explained that he spends Saturday nights here in prayer and fasting, allowing God to fill him with power for the Sunday morning services. Before deciding to build the beautiful four thousand-seat sanctuary the church uses for worship, Kim told me he spent two periods of twenty-one days each in prayer and fasting. In Korea he is not considered a spiritual giant. A study by Kim himself reveals that no Korean pastor spends under one hour a day in prayer, and that 47 percent of them spend two hours or more. A life-style of prayer is simply expected of Korean Christian leaders, and most of them meet those expectations.

Some of the Korean churches have purchased "prayer mountains." I understand there are about 100 of them in Korea. These are properties set up as prayer retreat centers. I visited one, Young Moon Prayer Mountain, which regularly holds prayer rallies attracting up to thirty thousand persons. It has a tabernacle which accommodates seven thousand.

But the Fasting Prayer Mountain of the Full Gospel Central Church is the largest and most active. Located at Osanri, just south of the demilitarized zone, it represents a fulfilled vision of Pastor Paul Yonggi Cho's mother-in-law, Jashil Choi, who founded it in 1973. Careful records are kept of all that happens at Prayer Mountain, again underscoring the crucial importance attached to prayer. The latest figures I have show that over 750 thousand visits are made in a year. A commercial bus company has scheduled hourly runs over the forty-five-minute route from Seoul. Many visitors just go to attend the revival-type services, but in a given year over eighty thousand individuals go specifically for prayer and fasting. A staff of no less than 130 full- and part-time ministers is on duty to instruct them in the correct method of fasting for periods of from one to forty days. The only restaurant is a fasting withdrawal service with scientifically-planned menus. Over 100 private individual prayer grottos have been dug into the mountain itself, and every one is occupied almost twenty-four hours a day. Construction is underway to increase the number to 500. Founder Jashil Choi says, "When we meet a difficult problem it is essential that we pray in all fervency and earnestness. With prayer and fasting we can cast Satan out, bring deliverance from bondage, and receive healing for our physical bodies."

When I visited Prayer Mountain recently, I was deeply impressed by the vast number of poor, oppressed, and afflicted there. It seemed that I was looking at the same kind of a crowd that would gather around Jesus in Galilee. The care for these people is a dramatic example of fulfilling the cultural mandate. The official scriptural motto of Prayer Mountain comes from Isaiah 58:6: "Is this not the fast that I have chosen; to loose the bond of wickedness, to undo the heavy burdens, to let the oppressed go free, and that you break every yoke?"

While such sustained and intense prayer life is not as yet a part of ordinary American Christianity, some great periods of revival here have been born out of prayer. The one which relates most to missions was the haystack prayer meeting of 1806. Samuel Mills, a student at Williams College in Massachusetts, knew what the life of prayer meant. He spent every Wednesday and Saturday afternoon in a student prayer group on the banks of the Hoosack River. One day in August the group was caught in a thunderstorm, so they took refuge under a haystack and held their meeting there. God led them to pray specifically for missions, touching off a chain of events which culminated in the famous Student Volunteer Movement. Historian Kenneth Scott Latourette says, "It was from this haystack meeting that the foreign missionary movement of the churches of the United States had an initial main impulse."

There now seems to be a promising trend in the United States toward a new depth of prayer life that has not characterized American churches recently. Some leaders, such as Vonette Bright of Campus Crusade, Evelyn Christenson, author of *What Happens When Women Pray?*, and Dick Eastman, director of the Change the World School of Prayer, are holding seminars which are helping thousands of Christian people to pray more and better. David Bryant of Inter-Varsity Missions is leading a new effort to promote "Concerts of Prayer" in major metropolitan areas "to mobilize a movement of prayer for spiritual awakening and world evangelization." Patrick Johnstone has published *Operation World: A Handbook for World Intercession* which includes prayer requests from every nation of the world. The Frontier Fellowship's *Daily Prayer Guide* is yet another tool to focus more effective prayer on missions.

What Kind of Power Do We Pray For?

Prayer by itself, of course, is not enough. What do we pray for? What do we expect God to do? Jesus told His disciples to "tarry in the city of Jerusalem until you are endued with power from on high" (Luke 24:49). As I look back over more than twenty-five years of professional involvement in missions, I have to say that I have seen very little of the literal New Testament power that Jesus was speaking of. The kind of power His disciples received when they tarried in Jerusalem is described in the rest of the book of Acts. It was the kind of power that the Apostle Paul wrote about after many fruitful years of missionary experience: "I will not dare to speak of any of those things which Christ has not accomplished through me, in word and deed to make the Gentiles obedient—in mighty signs and wonders, by the power of the Spirit" (Rom. 15:18-19).

Throughout my sixteen years of missionary experience in Bolivia I did not see any of these signs and miracles. Within the last couple of years I have been trying to figure out why this was so. I was trained by Inter-Varsity in college, then by Fuller Seminary. I was ordained by a Bible church and served under two thoroughly evangelical IFMA missions. I believed the Bible was the Word of God and could sign the strictest doctrinal statements. I moved in evangelical circles, attended evangelical conferences and lived an evangelical life-style. As such, like most evangelicals, I naturally heard much about the Holy Spirit. In fact, I taught a great deal about the Holy Spirit and about His power. As I think back on it I can't find that anything I taught was wrong. However, while there was nothing wrong, I now see that there may have been something missing.

One of my seminary professors was Harold Lindsell, former editor of *Christianity Today*. Our families have remained in touch through the years. Lindsell recently told me about some incidents in his own life that sound quite like incidents in the book of Acts. He now believes that New Testament power is available to Christians today. He has expressed these ideas in a book *The Holy Spirit in the Latter Days*. I said, "Harold, how come you never taught me that in the classes at Fuller?" He looked back at me and said, "I was deeply influenced by the Keswick tradition. We were taught that the power of the Holy Spirit was for living a holy life."

This is what I and most of my evangelical colleagues have been taught through the years. The power of the Spirit was not only for cleaning up the life but for witnessing and winning souls. When the news would come that a drunkard or dope addict would be saved, that was the power we expected. Harry R. Boer's notable book *Pentecost and Missions* stresses the crucial role of the power of the Holy Spirit in missions, but does not deal with signs, wonders, and miracles in our lives today. In a fine essay entitled "The Holy Spirit—The Power for World Mis sions," David Howard, now general secretary of the World Evangelical Fellowship, lists four ways this power is exercised: (1) filling men for power in witness, (2) giving gifts to the church for outreach, (3) choosing some for special outreach, and (4) guiding men in outreach. This is exactly where I have been in my thinking for most of my Christian life.

Why is it that we American evangelicals have not really believed in the immediate power of the Holy Spirit in miracles and wonders? Oh, most of us believed it intellectually because we read about it in the Bible. But it did not play much of a part, if any, in our daily lives or in our churches. I now think that a good deal of the problem is the pervasive influence of secular humanism in our American culture.

One of my colleagues at the Fuller School of World Mission is Paul G. Hiebert, a former Mennonite missionary to India. He helped me a great deal through an article he wrote for *Missiology* called, "The Flaw of the Excluded Middle." In it he points out that when John the Baptist's disciples asked Jesus whether He was the Messiah, Jesus did not give logical proofs but a power demonstration in healing the sick and casting out evil spirits. But Hiebert confesses that he became uneasy when he used to read this in India because "as a Westerner, I was used to presenting Christ on the basis of rational arguments, not by evidences of His power in the lives of people who were sick, possessed and destitute." He did believe in Christ's ability to confront evil spirits, but that, he says, "belonged in my mind to a separate world of the miraculous—far from ordinary everyday experience." Hiebert goes on to analyze our two-tiered Western world view which has "God confined to the supernatural, and the natural world operating for all practical purposes according to autonomous scientific laws," pointing out that for most of the peoples and cultures of today's world this is an odd way of looking at reality. Most people today, as in Jesus' day, expect the supernatural, whether forces of good or evil, to be active in ordinary everyday life.

Part of the challenge of reaching about 2.3 billion individuals in 16,750 unreached people groups is to adapt our message and ministry to their world view, not to expect them to accept ours. Our failure to do this in many cases has led us into a trap. Paul Hiebert makes the rather astounding observation that "Western Christian missions have been one of the greatest secularizing forces in history." As I look back I can now see how I, with a mixture of innocence and naivete, made my small contribution to this process in Bolivia.

Teaching Power in the Seminary Classroom

One of my consolations is that I am not alone. I previously mentioned that we now have nine full-time and several more part-time faculty members at the Fuller School of World Mission. We have talked together about this issue at great length. With the exception of one rather isolated incident where our dean, Paul Pierson, was involved in casting out a demon, our experience in seeing the supernatural power of God at work in everyday life was virtually nil. But we have no intention of maintaining the status quo. While none of us is categorized as a Pentecostal or charismatic, we nevertheless want to be open to whatever God desires to do. The founder of the school, Donald McGavran, says, "I do not come from a church background that emphasizes healing. In fact we have been a bit critical of it." But over the past decade or so his research on church growth revealed a close relationship between divine healing and church growth in some situations. McGavran now says, "The evidence I uncovered in country after country—and in North America as well—simply wouldn't permit me to hold my former point of view. And I may say that as I meditated on it, my biblical conviction also wouldn't permit it."

In his landmark volume *Christianity in Culture* Charles Kraft argues that if a missionary to Africa, who is thought of as a spokesperson for the true God, will not or cannot address the problem of illness effectively, the message will be regarded as an inadequate proclamation of Christian truth. Kraft points out that "illness is a matter of theological (not simply medical) understanding in virtually all cultures except those characterized by Western secularism." All this prompted him to make a statement in one of our faculty meetings: "We can no longer afford to send people back to the third world or out there for the first time without previously teaching them how to pray for the sick and cast out demons!"

One of our adjunct professors, John Wimber, who is pastor of Vineyard Christian Fellowship of Yorba Linda, California, came to us recently with a suggestion that we offer a course in Signs, Wonders, and Church Growth. I agreed to cosponsor the course with him, and early in

1982 we experimented with it. Eighty signed up for the
course and saw God do remarkable things right there in
the classroom. *Christian Life* magazine picked it up and
dedicated a whole issue to it in October, 1982. The following year enrollment jumped to 279 and the syllabus
expanded to a remarkable 250-page document. Wimber
regularly sees dramatic healings in his church which is now
running over three thousand in attendance. God has also
given him a unique ability to train others to pray for the
sick.

All of this means that we now are able to understand
more fully the dynamics behind much of the worldwide
church growth that was described in the first chapter. The
power has been around for a long time—it has just been
some of us who were not able to discern it. I now see how
important it is in fulfilling the Great Commission. As I
reread the Bible, I find that all five appearances of the
Great Commission (Matt. 28:18-20; Mark 16:15-18; Luke
24:47-49; John 20:21-22; and Acts 1:8) are accompanied
by promises of divine power. The Pentecostals, of course,
discovered this around the beginning of our century, and
their success in spreading the gospel has been outstanding. David Barrett, editor of the *World Christian Encyclopedia,* points out that Pentecostals, with 51 million, are the
largest distinct block of Protestants in the world today. He
further estimates that 11 million members of more traditional denominations also follow Pentecostal practices.

Let's take a closer look now at what has been happening behind the scenes in the areas of the most rapid spread
of the gospel which were mentioned in chapter 1.

God's Power in China

We now know that the church was growing tremendously in China while the bamboo curtain was still down. It
has grown from 1 million to at least 50 million. There are

now more evangelical Christians in China than in the United States. Many expert China watchers have been studying this growth and discovering the main reason for it. One of the common themes of their reports is the observation that in every province there has been a spontaneous outbreak of supernatural signs and wonders, sometimes even surpassing what we read about in the book of Acts.

David Adeney of Overseas Missionary Fellowship relates this power to prayer. "Conscious of their own weaknesses," Adeney says, "Chinese Christians follow the example of the early church and devote themselves to prayer. Many have believed because God has obviously heard the cry of His children, bringing deliverance in times of danger, in healing, and in freeing the demon possessed."

Jonathan Chao, director of the Chinese Church Research Center in Hong Kong, writes: "We have heard of all kinds of miracles. Everyone among Chinese Christians takes this for granted simply because there are so many miracles. The sick are healed. Terminal diseases such as cancer have been totally cured. There have been miracles of exorcising demons and the dead have been raised." Chao also relates this to prayer. While the Koreans hold dawn prayer meetings, Chinese hold evening prayer meetings. Many Chinese Christians according to Chao, attend prayer meetings in homes every evening of the week from 8:00 to 11:00.

Paul Kauffman, president of Asian Outreach, says, "The Church in China, for the most part, is well aware of the spiritual nature of the conflict. They know it is 'not by might nor by power, but by the Spirit of God' (Zechariah 4:6) that the church can fulfill its function in the world. Consequently, miracles, confrontation with evil spirits, and conquest over them is common among China's Christians, particularly in the house churches. In fact, it is this supernatural dimension, so often missing in the church in the West, that is *the most significant factor* in the growth of the Christian church in China."

David Wang, Kauffman's colleague and general director of Asian Outreach, has personally told me numerous stories about the supernatural working of God in China which are astounding. For example, Wang, a native of Shanghai who visits mainland China frequently, was asked by a Chinese family in New York if he would take a Bible to their son who was a young medical doctor in central China. Wang located the hospital where he worked, but when he met the doctor in his office, the doctor scribbled on a piece of paper that they should not talk there but that David was to come to his house later. That evening David Wang delivered the Bible and asked the doctor why he wrote his parents in New York and requested it.

The doctor said, "I have been an atheist and a Communist. I believed the party line. I've never been to a church. I've never talked to a Christian. I've never even see a Bible until tonight, much less read one. But I believe in God with all my heart."

Then he went on to tell about his encounter with God. "A few months ago a peasant woman arrived in the emergency room. As she was working in her commune, a huge rock fell on her chest and crushed her. The barefoot doctors in the commune could do nothing, so they sent her to the city. As soon as I saw her I knew there was nothing I could do either. Every bone in the left side of her chest was shattered. The x-rays showed that the broken ribs had pierced the lung and destroyed it.

"As I helped place the woman on her bed to die, I heard a faint whisper, and I put my ear down to listen closely. I thought she was unconscious, but I heard her whispering, 'Jesus, save me! Jesus, save me!' Nothing registered with me at the time, so I went home.

"The next morning I went back to the hospital and walked into this woman's ward. I could not believe my eyes! Instead of an empty bed, there she was sitting up and gulping down a bowl of rice soup. In my astonishment, I shouted at her: 'What are you doing?' The poor woman was so frightened she handed the bowl to me and said, 'I'm sorry, doctor. The nurse asked me if I was hungry, and I said yes!'

"At first I thought there must have been a mistake. But I checked her name and her work unit number. It was definitely the same woman. I rushed her back to the X-ray room and discovered that every bone had been perfectly healed overnight. The lung was functioning normally. I don't know much about Him, but I now believe in that woman's Jesus because I have seen His power. I'll read the Bible you brought me from cover to cover."

Wang now has reports of how God has subsequently used the peasant woman. She returned to her commune and began to preach Christ openly—with one X-ray picture in her left hand and the other in her right hand. Of 120 families in the commune, 80 had become Christians as of the last report.

Supernatural signs and wonders have become so powerful and widespread that the Communist government has begun to take steps to curtail them. For example, in Honan Province the government-related Three Self Church has published a list of "Ten Don'ts" that Christians in Central China should observe. The list contains items like this:

- Don't criticize the party and its policies in the name of preaching.
- Don't pretend to be a pastor or elder and conduct ordination or baptism or otherwise increase the number of believers.

- Don't pray every day; pray only on Sundays.
  And then, this revealing item:
- Don't pray for the sick or exorcise the demons.

India and Cambodia

I mentioned in chapter 1 that the great headhunting tribes of Northeast India are now largely Christian. A number of Christian leaders from those tribes now have their degrees in missiology from our school. Supernatural signs and wonders have been so common among those tribes that the leaders frequently forget to mention them. One of them, Robert Cunville, now serves as an evangelist in India with the Billy Graham Evangelistic Association. He relates a fascinating story of the power of God among the Nishi tribe.

A Nishi government official's son had become critically ill and was dying. The town doctor was away. The government official went to the local pharmacist who told him that his son was beyond medical help. "Why not sacrifice to your gods?" the pharmacist asked.

"I have," the official responded. "I have sacrificed my best goat and water buffalo."

Then the pharmacist said, "Why not try the Christian's God—Jesus Christ?"

The official sadly turned away and went home. When he arrived he saw that the neighbors were going into his house and he knew the worst had happened. His son had died. His wife was in tears, and he was deeply moved with emotion. Then something stirred inside the official and he said out loud, "Jesus, I don't know who you are, but I heard you have power to raise the dead. My son died only a few hours ago. If you raise up my son, I promise that my family and I will worship you forever."

No sooner had he finished the prayer than the dead

boy's eyes began to flicker. Soon they opened and before long he was completely well. The official's family kept their promise and became dedicated Christians. Soon hundreds of other families in the area had also accepted Christ as Saviour and Lord.

In nearby Cambodia (Kampuchea) the accelerated growth of the church started when the Communists took over and hundreds of thousands of Cambodians fled to the refugee camps across the border in Thailand. Those who didn't make it were brutally murdered by the Communist soldiers.

Among a group of about 100 Cambodians who were trying to make their way to the Thai border was a nineteen-year-old girl named Kham Put. For several days they had eluded the Communist patrols, and they were just a few hours away from the border. But between the group and freedom lay a jungle valley thickly covered with thorns. Darkness was falling and they were barefoot so they had to make camp. No sooner did they settle down than their sentinels heard the noises of a Communist patrol coming their way. By then it was pitch-black with no moon and no stars. They were trapped.

Suddenly they looked up and saw an eerie glow. Hundreds of fireflies appeared in their camp and a strange man was surrounded by their light. The man and the fireflies led them down the path through the thorns and to safety in Thailand.

Some days later in the refugee camp, Kham Put was invited to a Christian meeting. She had never heard the gospel. But when she went inside the structure being used as a meeting place, her eyes widened and she pointed to a picture on the wall. "I know that old man," she said. "He is the one who came with the fireflies and led us through the jungle to freedom." Kham Put was pointing to a picture of Jesus!

Central America

One of the flash points of church growth worldwide is in Central America. As has been mentioned, Guatemala, for example, is now 25 percent evangelical and the churches continue to grow rapidly.

Enrique Zone, a student of mine, is now president of the *Facultad de Teologia,* a training school for Hispanic ministers near Los Angeles, sponsored by the International Church of the Foursquare Gospel. In his experience throughout Latin America he has often seen the power of God in full operation. One of the outstanding examples took place in the town of Santa Rosa in Guatemala.

Back in the 1960s a serious drought had come upon Santa Rosa. A state of emergency was declared. Horses and cattle were dying. The government sent special study teams to try to solve the problem. Wells were being dug all over, but they came up dry. The Roman Catholic church held special masses.

A small evangelical church called *Principe de Paz* was located in Santa Rosa. The believers also had a special prayer meeting to ask God for wisdom, since they too were being destroyed by the drought. The Holy Spirit's power began to operate in their midst during the prayer meeting, and they received a prophecy directly from God. It said, "You are to dig a well in the pastor's backyard."

If their faith had not been strong they would not have accepted it as a legitimate prophecy. It made no sense because the pastor's house was on top of a hill. Everyone knew that the last place to dig a well was on the top of a hill. But they launched out in faith and began digging the well.

The unbelievers gathered around and mocked them. They thought the evangelicals had lost their minds. After a few days of digging they struck a huge boulder, and they were discouraged. They wondered if they had interpreted the prophecy correctly. Some of the believers quit, but others kept working on the boulder. Eventually they were able to move it, and as soon as they did a strong stream of pure water gushed forth. They had struck an artesian well, and the village was saved!

From that point on, everyone in the village had to go to the pastor's house for water. There was always a deacon there to welcome the people and to say to them, "He who drinks of this water shall thirst again, but he who drinks of the water that Christ gives shall never thirst again."

It was the beginning of a great harvest. Hundreds were saved that year. The Catholic church closed down for lack of members. The *Principe de Paz* Church has one thousand members, and water is still coming out of the well.

Ethiopia and South Africa

One of the fastest growing Lutheran churches of all time is the Mekane Yesus Lutheran Church of Ethiopia. In the last two years it has grown from 100 thousand to 500 thousand members. A friend of mine, Professor Tormod Engelsviken of the Free Faculty of Theology in Oslo, Norway, recently handed me the report of a scholarly study made by Lutheran researchers there. They were attempting to understand the causes of such unprecedented church growth.

Much to their amazement, they found that between 60 and 80 percent of the new Lutheran believers had been attracted to Christianity through either direct experience or firsthand observation of the supernatural power of God in signs and wonders. Engelsviken said, "We thought they were responding because we were preaching the correct Lutheran doctrine of justification by faith. But now we know that it was not doctrine as such that was attracting their attention. It was the direct power of God in their everyday life that made the difference."

Then he told me one of the numerous stories coming out of Ethiopia. In Awasa, one of the provincial capitals of southern Ethiopia, a church leader had been arrested by the Communist police. He was interrogated and punished. Then the Communist official said, "Curse the enemies of the revolution and I will let you go." The Christian knew that as he said it he would be expected to raise his left fist in the Communist salute.

"I cannot do it," he responded. "Jesus told us to bless our enemies, not to curse them."

"Then you will grasp this high tension wire!" the Communist said. A bare electrical wire was held in front of him.

The Christian leader said, "In the name of Jesus!" and grabbed the wire with his bare hand. At once the whole town went into a blackout! The man was unhurt. Instead of his left fist, he raised both hands, smiled at the Communist and said, "Praise the Lord!"

On the other end of the African continent, in South Africa, God is doing amazing things. Churches are springing up like mushrooms in a cow pasture. Two South African Pentecostal leaders, Johan Engelbrecht and Christiaan De Wet, just took degrees in missiology at our school. Their denomination, the Apostolic Faith Mission Church, is the largest Pentecostal church in South Africa reporting 2 million members. The story of how that church started is awesome.

It started through a missionary named John G. Lake. Just after the turn of the century, Lake was touched by God in the Azusa Street revival in Los Angeles and called to be a missionary to South Africa. He obeyed God, went to South Africa, and began preaching the gospel. But no one attended his meetings. He became deeply discouraged. He began a prolonged period of fasting and prayer.

On the twenty-first day of his fast, he was walking

down one of the main streets of Johannesburg when a horse pulling a carriage stumbled and broke its leg. It was thrashing around in the street and a crowd gathered. The policeman had a conference with the owner and they decided that the horse should be shot and put out of its misery. Just as the policeman aimed his gun, John G. Lake felt inspired by God. He walked up to the policeman, and said, "Don't shoot that horse. God has told me that He wants to heal him."

The bystanders were aghast. Lake stretched out his hand and began to pray for the horse's broken leg. Soon the horse calmed down, and then got to its feet. The leg was healed and the horse pulled the carriage down the street.

The people came to Lake's meetings that night! And they kept coming. From that point over the next five years, John G. Lake saw a new church planted in South Africa on the average of every three days!

The stories that I have told have been selected from many, many more. There is no question in my mind that the power of God is just as strong today as it was in the first century. Jesus is the same yesterday, today and forever. His words, "Tarry . . . until you are endued with power from on high," are words for all of us. I am increasingly convinced that the more we tune into this power, the more rapidly we will be able to complete the task of world evangelization.

Do Something Now!

1. Get a copy of *Operation World: A Handbook for World Intercession* by Patrick J. Johnstone, available in your Christian bookstore or from STL Books, Box 28, Waynesboro, Georgia 30830. This is the best book on relating prayer to missions.

2. Send $4.95 plus $1.00 for postage and handling to

Christian Life Magazine, 396 E. St. Charles Road, Wheaton, Illinois 60187 and request a copy of *Signs and Wonders Today.* This study book tells how the first course in Signs, Wonders and Church Growth came about at Fuller Seminary and what the results were. It is divided into thirteen sections with group discussion study questions at the end of each section. This is one of the best introductions to the whole area of supernatural power, with articles by John Wimber, David Hubbard, Donald McGavran, Peter Wagner, Christian De Wet, Eddie Gibbs, and many more.

3. Consider ordering and listening to the series of thirty cassette tapes on healing by John Wimber. They are quite expensive, but worth the money. Each of the four sets is accompanied by a well-designed study guide. Write Vineyard Ministries International, P.O. Box 65, Placentia, CA 92670 or call toll free 1-800-824-7888 (in California 1-800-852-7777).

4. Inquire to see if any churches in your area have a regular healing ministry. If so, visit the churches, talk to the pastors or lay leaders, and discuss your findings with a study group.

Eight

Asking the Right Questions

In a field developing as rapidly as missions, at times it seems difficult for a person once removed from the inner circles to keep up on what is going on. Even some missionaries themselves out on the front lines of the battle, exhausted by monsoons, mosquitoes, and malaria, find they have little energy or inclination to attempt to read the journals and relate to the intellectual currents swirling around the centers of missiology.

It would expand this book unduly to cover the major issues in missions in chapter-length essays. In this chapter, then, I will deal with five of the major issues in condensed form. Each of them will undoubtedly continue to be a focal point of intelligent missiological discussion for many years to come.

Redefining the "Indigenous Church"

Planting new churches is one of the chief responsibilities of missionaries. The word *baptize* in the Great Commission is commonly taken as a mandate to organize newborn disciples into local churches. Although this is a universally accepted principle, the resulting churches take on a wide variety of forms. This could be good or it could be bad. Much depends on whether the new churches are truly indigenous.

The concept of the indigenous church, as applied to those churches planted by missionaries all over the world, has traditionally included three aspects. The churches are to be: self-governing, self-supporting, and self-propagating.

Until recently it has been assumed that when a church exhibits these three characteristics it is thereby "indigenous." Some missiologists, however, have now begun to question the adequacy of the three-self definition of the indigenous church. They do not think the current definition is *wrong*, they only contend that it is *incomplete*.

What is the problem? The problem is that all the three selfs could be in full operation but the church could still be a foreign institution, considered by the nationals as a weird and irrelevant curiosity in their society.

A church like this is not truly indigenous since the cultural aspect has not adequately been dealt with. A whole new breed of missionary anthropologists is making us aware that a church planted on the mission field should so take on the characteristics of that culture that it is considered homegrown, or else it may never become a healthy, growing church.

There are some aspects of Christianity that must not yield to any culture all. These are called supracultural elements. If people are in the habit of sacrificing human beings to the rain god, for example, this must stop.

Drunkenness and debauchery have to go when the Holy Spirit takes over. Devil worship cannot continue. Adultery must fade in the white light of Christian ethics.

But watch out! Be sure you do not fall into the trap of defining adultery or other things the Bible condemns in terms that are also bound to your own culture. Some missionaries who planted churches among polygamous peoples may have done just that. All agree that adultery means sexual relations outside of marriage. But Western missionaries were not brought up in their culture to believe that a man could be *legally married* to more than one woman. Many third-world cultures, however, make provision for that. The current opinion among missionary anthropologists is that many missions may have been hasty in insisting that a converted man leave all his wives but one before he could be baptized. This does not mean that they necessarily *approve* polygamy. They do suggest, however, that the transition could have been smoother, following more indigenous patterns. They contrast the phenomenal growth of the African independent churches to some slower-growing foreign churches in order to reinforce their point.

Don't forget, churches aren't ends in themselves. *Baptizing* is only one of the helping verbs, useful and necessary in accomplishing the Great Commission goal of making disciples, but not an end in itself. The final product of our efforts must be nothing less than disciples. Some churches are useful in making disciples, but unfortunately some are not. A major crippling factor in some churches is their lack of cultural relevance.

One of the outstanding examples might be the Christian church among Jewish people. A great deal of study is now being concentrated on discovering why conversions have been so infrequent among the Jews. Preliminary evidence indicates that the problem may lie in the area of cul-

tural relevance. Many suspect that the hangup of the Jews
may not be nearly so much theological as cultural. Implicit
in much previous missionary work among the Jews has
been the unspoken requirement that if Jews want to be
saved they must be willing to become like Gentiles and join
Gentile churches.

This is a reversal of the problem in the New Testament
church. There the Judaizers insisted that Gentiles become
Jews in order to be saved (Acts 15:1). Today some "genti-
lizers" seem to have arisen. Is it really necessary for a Jew
even to become a "Christian" in order to be saved? After
all, the believers in the Jerusalem church were not called
Christians, but *disciples* or followers "of the Way" (Acts
9:2). Only later on in Antioch, when Hellenists and Gentiles began coming into the church, were the believers
first called *Christians* (Acts 11:26). The Jewish law cer-
tainly does not earn salvation, but could a person believe
in Jesus as Messiah and still continue to keep the law?
Could a born-again believer worship on Saturday and keep
a kosher kitchen?

The Messianic Jewish Movement, which gained so
much strength during the seventies, would tend to answer
those questions in the affirmative. Messianic synagogues
have been springing up and providing ways that Jews can
become followers of Jesus without breaking cultural ties
with their own Jewish communities. One of the leaders of
the movement, Philip Goble, author of *Everything You
Need to Grow a Messianic Synagogue,* has recently turned
his attention to approaching Muslims in a similar way. He
has gathered a team of Muslim experts to look into ways
and means of establishing Messianic mosques. If Muslims
are accustomed to take their shoes off when they go into a
holy place and to worship kneeling on the floor instead of
sitting on a pew, why shouldn't they be encouraged to do
so?

The technical term for this process is "contextualization." It means that, to the degree possible without violating supracultural biblical principles, aspects of Christian life and ministry—such as life-style, theological formulations, worship patterns, music, ethics, leadership structures, and others, should be free to take on the forms of each new culture which Christianity enters. This is not easy. Techniques of contextualization are fairly well advanced, but a great deal more needs to be done. As it is worked out and applied with wisdom, however, the resulting indigenous church will be much more authentically *indigenous* than many have been in the past. And presumably this will open the doors to an even more accelerated spread of the gospel worldwide.

The Syndrome of Church Development

It is so easy for a good missionary to get sidetracked! In fact it can even happen to a whole mission, and it has.

One of the most common ways of getting sidetracked is to fall into what I like to call the *syndrome of church development*. If I were to make a catalog of missionary maladies, I would put this one high on the list. It cripples more missionaries than hepatitis, dysentery, and malaria put together.

When missionaries first go to the fourth world to preach the gospel and bring men and women to Christ, there is no danger of the syndrome of church development, mainly because there is no church as yet. The missionaries have their priorities right: they concentrate on those people who do not yet know Christ. But as soon as some are baptized, and as soon as a church is organized, they need to watch out. They can easily get so fascinated by the new little church that they forget why they went to the mission field in the first place.

The little church has so many needs. Although most

missionaries know they shouldn't be paternalistic, they have a difficult time suppressing their desire to shower an abundance of love and care on the newborn babes. The new believers are hungry for spiritual things; they need counseling to straighten out some of life's tangled problems; they want Bible teaching. Leaders need to be trained; literature must be produced in the vernacular; a church building is waiting to be constructed; someone who is trustworthy should be instructed to handle church finances. The believers need to be warned of heresy, taught the Lord's prayer and the Apostles' Creed, and instructed in witnessing. A Sunday School has to be organized. They have to learn the hymns, and someone needs to accompany congregational singing with musical instruments; they are poor and need financial help; the farmers could increase production with a little more agricultural know-how; and when they get sick someone has to take them to the doctor. The items in this list could easily be doubled or tripled. Even in a small church they add up to much more than one missionary can ever hope to do.

It happens so often, though. Missionaries begin to get deeply involved in church affairs. They know they should trust the Holy Spirit to fill the new believers, to give them spiritual gifts, to lead them into all truth (John 14:26), but they feel a need to provide a little boost. So far, so good. New believers do need some attention. Only irresponsible evangelists would bring people to Christ and then abandon them. But taking care of new churches can easily become habit-forming. A small dose of parental care is good, but when it becomes compulsive paternalism, when missionaries find themselves addicted, they have tumbled into the syndrome of church development.

Few things can quench missionary effectiveness as thoroughly as the syndrome of church development. The goal of good missionary strategy is to make disciples. But, as we have seen, disciples cannot be made in the *church*—they are made only in the *world*. Missionaries who let themselves get pulled out of the world and involved in developing the church are reducing the total effectiveness of the missionary society in fulfilling the Great Commission. This has become so much the pattern in some missionary societies that they no longer even call missionaries by that name. They call them "fraternal workers"! Missions becomes interchurch aid.

Take a close look at your favorite mission. List in parallel columns the names of the workers who are engaged in winning people to Christ and planting new churches as over against those who are developing the church. Most missions will be so overbalanced in the second column that you will immediately see they have fallen into the syndrome of church development.

This not only reduces effectiveness in making disciples, but, ironically, it frequently may hinder church development itself. There is almost an inverse relationship between paternalism and church quality. The more paternalism, the worse the church. This is one of the reasons why on many mission fields the so-called "indigenous movements," meaning the churches that have developed with little or no foreign missionary influence, are growing much faster than the non-indigenous ones. It also may provide at least part of the explanation of the phenomenon that in some cases, such as in China, when the missionaries leave, the church grows more vigorously than ever.

The objective for mission agencies should be to plant the church in a new people group, allow it to get rooted, and as quickly as possible take hands off the church, trust the Holy Spirit to guide it, and then move on to the next unreached people group. At this point a very serious problem has arisen in recent years. Many mission agencies have declared themselves to be servants of the national church, which means that within the territorial boundaries of a given country the mission does only what the national church allows it to do. Donald McGavran feels that adopting the policy has tended to put shackles on the mission agencies and divert their attention from the unreached. He says, "World evangelization and the discipling of all the peoples of planet Earth is so clearly Christ's will, the task so many-faceted, and today's technological advances so numerous that *unshackling the missionary societies is urgent.* We must be free to proclaim Christ and to disciple the nations in any way possible."

If the national church has a burning desire to reach out, and if it places a high priority on dispatching missionaries—whether their own or from abroad—to disciple the unreached peoples, no problem should exist. But this is all too frequently not the case. Professor Harvie Conn of Westminster Seminary tells the story of how he once sincerely attempted to motivate a group of pastors at a conference in Uganda to engage in foreign missions. His proposal was greeted with sustained laughter. In their minds, frontier missions was a responsibility of Westerners, not of themselves.

The question arises, then, are evangelistic and church planting missionaries still needed? Some do not think so. I have before me a recent list of openings in a respected EFMA mission agency which will go unnamed. Of fifty different categories, only two relate to evangelism, both focused on youth. The rest of the categories include, among others, agronomists, music teachers, nurses, automobile mechanics, secretaries, electronics professors, and ecologists. In contrast, another EFMA mission, OMS International, still stresses the evangelistic task and has set a goal of planting 200 new churches in one year. Wesley Duewel, of OMS International, reports that "OMS has more than 60 evangelistic teams helping Jesus build His church by planting new congregations. These work mainly in new villages or new sections of cities where no Christian church exists." Bill O'Brien, an executive with the Southern Baptist Foreign Mission Board, the world's largest, says that their major effort for personnel mobilization still needs to be "an unprecedented number of persons who can serve as church planters and field evangelists." I agree with Duewel and O'Brien. Evangelistic missionaries will be needed as long as any people groups are yet unreached. Jesus has not yet told us to stop praying for laborers to go into the harvest fields.

Diagnostic Research in Evangelism

In a way I hate to report it, but it is sadly true that the mission fields of the world are overloaded with evangelistic programs that are not functioning properly. Sadder yet, many people deeply involved in them don't even realize the fact. The symptoms of the disease are effectively masked by a great amount of activity, long hours of work, flamboyant advertising, high-pressure spiritual exercises for the believers, large expenditures of funds, and all other things that add up to a superevangelistic program. The program *should* bring multitudes of unsaved people to Christ, but it *doesn't*!

In many of these programs, believe it or not, the results are not even tested. It is just *assumed* that all the hard work has paid off. Sometimes the verse, "My word . . . shall not return to Me void" (Isa. 55:11), is quoted as a device to avoid the responsibility of checking results against investments.

Almost accidentally I began to do diagnostic research on one of our massive evangelistic programs in Bolivia some years ago. Along with all the others involved, I had simply assumed that large numbers of disciples had been made as a result. Had we not invested over a year of time?

Were not thousands of church members trained in personal evangelism? Did not multitudes of believers meet weekly in cells for earnest prayer? Were not radio and literature used extensively? Did not the visitation, the congresses, and the campaigns bring a large percentage of Bolivia's population under the hearing of the gospel? Were we not exhausted when it was all through? Did we not record over twenty thousand decisions for Christ?

The answer to all these questions was yes. But we were foolish enough to believe that we also had effectively accomplished the goals of Strategy I—*making disciples.* When we undertook diagnostic research some years later, however, we discovered that the growth rate of the major churches involved had actually declined rather than increased! Subsequent research in other countries has shown that Bolivia was not an exception to the rule. It was bad news, just as it is when your doctor's diagnostic research shows that you need an operation. But in spite of the pain you're glad that he discovered the disease now rather than letting it kill you.

Good diagnostic research can still save many of our evangelistic programs, if it is carried out with courage and skill. Theological seminaries need to include such research methodologies in their curricula. If only the current fad of holding nationwide, regional, and even world congresses on evangelism could be harnessed to teach diagnostic skills to church leaders across the board, the cause of evangelism and missions would be advanced in a spectacular way.

Quite a bit of work was done on methodologies for diagnostic research during the seventies. Without question, Vergil Gerber of the Evangelical Missions Information Service was the chief promoter of this approach to making evangelism more effective during the past decade. He held workshops in over fifty nations and wrote a manual which has been translated and published in over forty languages. As a result, the level of awareness of the need for hard-nosed evaluation of whether or not evangelistic programs are succeeding has risen tremendously around the world.

I myself had the privilege of working with Gerber in the early years. Toward the end of the decade I then teamed up with Bob Waymire, a skillful researcher with Overseas Crusades. Waymire and I developed *The Church Growth Survey Handbook* in an attempt to draw together the best current technology for diagnostic work and present it in a useful form. This forty-page manual has already been used fairly extensively and is providing a uniform basis of researching and reporting the growth of the church around the world.

Among other things, *The Church Growth Survey Handbook* introduces a very helpful set of four diagnostic categories which were formulated in a two-year consortium of research specialists from the major American denominations who met at Hartford Seminary. In any given situation the growth of a given local church or group of churches will be influenced to one degree or another by each of the four ingredients:

First, national contextual factors. This refers to conditions which prevail throughout a whole nation or sometimes throughout a significant region. For example, national contextual factors are very important for understanding contemporary church growth in North Korea or in Saudi Arabia. They help explain why Japanese people were very open to the gospel for seven years after World War II. They include such things as migrations, wars, persecutions, religious attitudes, politics, economic conditions, etc.

Second, local contextual factors. This refers to the immediate town, village, tribe, or section of the city where the church is located. The growth of churches there will be affected by housing patterns, changing neighborhoods, rate of unemployment, urbanization, population growth, etc.

Third, national institutional factors. This refers to decisions, policies and programs developed and promoted by the whole denomination or judicatory or mission agency which will influence the growth or nongrowth of all the churches which pertain to it.

Fourth, local institutional factors. This refers to the situation within a given congregation. Important local institutional factors include the quality of pastoral leadership, the mobilization of the laypeople for ministry, development of small group structures, facilities, spirituality, stewardship, and many other aspects of local church life.

Use of these diagnostic categories, plus others combined with proper statistics and graphing techniques, can allow any pastor or church leader to size up the situation of a church or cluster of churches and intelligently make a faith projection for where God wants the Church to go in the future.

Short-Term Missionary Service

A generation ago, almost everyone who volunteered for missionary service assumed they were offering a lifetime to the work. Nowadays, however, an increasing number of young people hesitate to make a hasty commitment for life. The new generation has been accused of being less spiritual. I doubt that. Perhaps they are simply wiser and more cautious than their fathers. Besides, they have some new options open to them.

According to the latest reports, of the fifty-three thousand-some North American missionaries, about seventeen thousand or one-third are short-term missionaries. But they are coming and going constantly, so the estimate of the number on the field at any one time is about eighty-five hundred. The average length of service is nineteen months, with terms ranging from a month or two to five years. Most but not all short-termers are young people. Older people also, some at mid-career and some at retirement, are volunteering for short-term service in increasing numbers.

There are several ways to do it, but I like to categorize short-term workers as follows:

Skilled workers. Men and women with particular skills are accepted by a mission society for a stated task. They know their job description before they leave for the field, and they also know how long they expect to serve.

Short-term service provides a magnificent opportunity for young people, or older ones for that matter, to test their missionary gift. One couple came to our missionary children's school for a two-year term. After four months they decided they had the missionary gift and applied for full career membership in the mission. Another couple was sent to the school for one year by their own church missionary committee. Before the year was over they discovered that they did *not* have the missionary gift, although they had made a good contribution to the school. In my opinion, the test was successful in both cases. The Lord spoke to the latter couple as clearly as to the former. Now they are happily settled in the U.S.A., active in their church, better Christians because of their year's experience on the mission field, and free of any nagging guilt feelings that they might have had if they had not tested their gifts.

The major drawback in the case of short-term skilled workers is that they cannot take time for a full course of language and culture learning. But there is much they can do in English. Hostesses for guest homes, farm managers, airplane pilots, school teachers, dentists, house-parents, radio technicians, typists, accountants, cooks, and scores of other jobs are open to qualified short-term workers who know only one language and culture.

Furthermore, some rather exciting new research and experimentation indicates that learning a new language and culture might not be all as difficult as we Americans have assumed. Many of us took language courses in high school or college and considered them disasters. The experience contributed to an ingrained mental block against all language study. But an ingenious couple, Professors Tom and Betty Sue Brewster, have developed a viable alternative which they call LAMP (Language Acquisition Made Practical). This approach is designed to help language learners to get around the mental block and to learn a new language and culture much as we all learned our own when we were children.

Interns. Interns are workers who are building a year of foreign service into their training programs. Typically, interns will take off one year from Bible school or seminary to become involved in missionary work. Often they will receive academic credit for their involvement.

Since the year is an integral part of training, the program for interns is often developed not so much according to what the intern will contribute to the mission's work as to what the mission can contribute to the intern's training. It often works both ways, however.

Summer students. More and more Christian young people are spending their summers on the mission field. Some are sent by mission boards, some by their schools, some by their churches or youth groups, and some just go to visit friends and relatives there.

Some missions design their programs in order to put the summer students to work. They may distribute tracts, hack a dugout canoe, type a book manuscript, or paint a campground. I have some reservations about this approach, however. While summer students undoubtedly should be assigned some unskilled labor during their time on the field, this should not be their only objective. In addition to accomplishing something for the mission, they should have at least an equal opportunity for a full and realistic exposure to as many aspects of missionary life as possible. They should gain as complete an orientation to native life as they can in the short time available, and they should take home a positive impression of missionary work.

Above all, they should be tuned in to the need for testing to see whether they have the missionary gift as was explained in chapter 3. Even a brief exposure like this will be sufficient for many to reach an intelligent conclusion.

Tentmakers. The term *tentmaker* comes from the Apostle Paul who, besides being the greatest missionary of all time, had also mastered the skill of tentmaking. At least some of the time he was serving as a missionary he supported himself with his secular profession. Christians who go out to other cultures today, but who support themselves rather than expecting to receive support from a church or mission agency, are known as tentmakers. Not all are short-termers; some make it a career.

J. Christy Wilson, Jr., author of *Today's Tentmakers,* points out that noted historic figures such as Marco Polo and Christopher Columbus can be understood as a type of tentmaking missionary. And also none other than William Carey, known as the father of the modern missionary movement, was a self-supporting missionary. The tradition has good historical as well as biblical precedent.

Generally speaking, there are two kinds of tentmaking missionaries. One kind, like William Carey, goes with the primary motivation of making the gospel known and then does whatever is necessary to survive while doing that. Another kind includes those people who go primarily because of a work assignment and then as they are able they share the gospel with others. Wilson's opinion is that "both types can render great service to the Lord."

One of the agencies associated with the U.S. Center for World Mission in Pasadena, California is the Overseas Counseling Service led by Donald Hamilton, who for many years directed the Association of Church Missions Committees. Hamilton points out that tentmaking can get people into many situations around the world where conventional missionaries are excluded. He is tooled to make it happen for those interested.

Theological Education by Extension

Although it is impossible to do justice to the vast subject of theological education by extension in a couple of pages, this would not be an up-to-date picture of missions without it. TEE, as it is called for short, started in Guatemala in 1962 and since then has spread not only around Latin America but throughout the world. Without doubt, it is now one of the most significant aspects of modern missions, and TEE will continue to provide an outstanding challenge for missionary teachers for a decade or two to come.

The need for rethinking theological education on the mission field came when some diagnostic research was done over a decade ago. It was discovered at that time that the traditional pattern of two to four years in a residence institution was not meeting the needs for ministerial training in many parts of the third world. For one thing, churches there were growing much too fast for seminaries and Bible schools to keep up. For another, the maintenance of the institution was too expensive for some local economies to support. Only substantial subsidies from abroad could sustain the schools. Many workers, missionaries and nationals alike, have long since realized that pro-

longed subsidies may sometimes induce unhealthy dependence on the part of the nationals and a spirit of paternalism on the part of the missionaries.

In many situations in the third world, new churches are
populated with first-generation converts. Among them are
gifted adult leaders who are obviously called to pastor the
church. But they have families and occupations and social
responsibilities which tie them to their present locations.
Chances of their being able to pull up stakes and attend a
residence institution for ministerial training are extremely
slim. Especially to provide training for this special kind of
person, many TEE programs have been developed.
Rather than insisting that all students come to the institution, systems have now been designed to take the training
to the students.

Many mission specialists believe that leadership selection and training is the single most crucial issue in the
spread of the gospel throughout the world today. Some
fine programs for TEE training have been set up by Kenneth Mulholland at Columbia Bible College, by Bobby Clin-
ton at the Fuller School of World Mission, by Lois McKin-
ney at the Wheaton Graduate School, and at other
seminaries. Patricia Harrison travels to all continents on
behalf of the World Evangelical Fellowship to provide skillful consultation for TEE.

I just happened to look at a recent list of personnel
needs for the missions of the IFMA. Specific mention is
made of the need for TEE workers by Africa Inland Mission, Arctic Missions, Gospel Missionary Union, Greater
Europe Mission, International Missions, South America
Mission, SIM International, and The Evangelical Alliance
Mission. Undoubtedly many other TEE positions with
other missions are open under listings such as leadership
training, Bible school teaching, theological education, and
others.

Because of its strategic importance, TEE ministry is one of the most challenging and fulfilling opportunities for missionaries today. I hope that many who read this will take it as a serious burden of prayer.

Do Something Now!

This has been a chapter which touches on several crucial aspects of contemporary missions. Here are some things you can do to continue to expand your own interests and involvement:

1. Join the Global Church Growth Book Club. In order to do this, you subscribe to *Global Church Growth,* "the only worldwide missiological magazine dedicated exclusively to Great Commission Mission," as its own introduction states. Every bimonthly issue will bring you the announcement of a new Global Church Growth Book Club selection plus news of other significant books in the field of missions. These books, in turn, are offered at a discount from the William Carey Library, and you buy only the ones you wish. Send $6.00 for a year's subscription to *Global Church Growth,* Box 66, Santa Clara, California 95052. For further information write Global Church Growth Book Club, Box 40129, Pasadena, California 91104.

2. Read the following books:

Mission-Church Dynamics by W. Harold Fuller (William Carey Library). This is the most complete account of how thinking has developed on the issue of mission-church relations and it outlines the options that must be considered.

Today's Tentmakers by J. Christy Wilson, Jr. (Tyndale House Publishers). This presents all the aspects of ministries for professionals who wish to go to the fields for short- or long-terms and support themselves while there.

The Church Growth Survey Handbook by Bob Waymire and C. Peter Wagner (Global Church Growth). Send $3.00

to Global Church Growth, Box 66, Santa Clara, California 95052 for a copy of this manual. Experiment with diagnosis by using it on your local church.

3. Take a serious independent study course. *Perspectives on the World Christian Movement* is a course that even can be arranged for college credit if you like. It consists of a magnificent 864-page *Reader,* edited by Ralph Winter and Steve Hawthorne, which brings together in one place key selections from numerous outstanding mission leaders, plus an accompanying 170-page study guide. This will lay a basis of understanding of world missions that will remain with you for life. For information write: Career Foundations, 1605 Elizabeth Street, Pasadena, California 91104.

Nine
Full Circle: Third-World Missions

God never intended missions to stop, at least until this age is over and Jesus returns.

That's why all the talk about the age of missions being over and about missionaries being no longer needed or wanted is nonsense. More missionaries than ever before should be moving out to the fields of the world if Christians are going to follow God's game plan.

One of the problems is that we have tended to see missions as a straight line rather than as a circle. We have foolishly supposed that missions has a starting point and an ending point and that the job can be completed in a given period of time. If you consider Christ's second coming as the end point, all right. But we can't live as though He's coming tomorrow, although it may well be that He will. In the meantime, God expects us to live and work as though

He were *not* coming. That means we need to continue and even increase our missionary efforts. There are still 16,750 people groups to be reached with the gospel. We need to view Christian missions as a continuous cycle, turning around and around with no foreseeable end in sight.

What Color Are Missionaries' Feet?

Several times in this book I have quoted the missionary passage in Romans 10. I have stressed the evangelistic mandate to preach the gospel, and I have stressed the need to send missionaries to do it. As this happens, we can then say with God: "How beautiful are the feet of those who preach the gospel of peace, who bring glad tidings of good things" (Rom. 10:15).

Now when you think of all those missionary feet going out, what color feet do you see?

Probably white!

No argument. It is a fact of life that the bulk of the missionary work up to now has been done by white Westerners. When you think of missionaries, you think of Americans or Englishmen or Canadians or Europeans or Australians or New Zealanders. The image is only natural because these people come from the countries where Christianity has been most deeply rooted throughout the centuries.

But no longer! The largest church in the world, for example, is not in Europe or in the U.S.A., but in Seoul, Korea. The Christian and Missionary Alliance Church has more members in Indonesia than in the U.S.A. Statistics show that by the turn of the century a full 60 percent of the world's Christians will be found in the third world. Within the next few decades the worldwide Christian center of gravity will have shifted to Africa. Christianity is no longer a white man's religion. Hallelujah! This means that the Christian missionary enterprise has been much more successful than William Carey or David Livingstone or Robert Morrison could have imagined in their fondest dreams.

One of the results of this new fact of world Christianity is that the feet of all those missionaries marching out with the message of Jesus Christ are changing color. Not that there are fewer white feet—heaven forbid! But in the closing years of the twentieth century these white feet will be joined by a dramatically increasing number of brown, black, red and yellow feet. In fact, my own educated guess is that by the end of the century there will be at least as many missionaries from the third world out on the field as missionaries from the traditional Western nations.

Missions 360 Degrees

This had to happen because missions are best not conceived of as a straight line—Westerners to the third world, period. Missions are best conceptualized as a circle, and God delights in 360-degree missions.

Here are the quadrants in the full circle of missionary activity:

• 90-degree missions—the mission sends out missionaries to a certain people group to preach the gospel, win men and women to Christ, and plant Christian churches.

• 180-degree missions—the seed of the Word bears fruit, people are saved, and a new church is planted. The new church is still under mission supervision and care.

• 270-degree missions—the church gains its autonomy, it begins to take care of its own affairs, and the mission either stays under a partnership agreement or moves elsewhere. Most of our mission programs today have been 270-degree programs. Some missions have even pulled out of the field when they turned the church over to the nationals, arguing that they had "worked themselves out of a job." This is simply another, less obvious, variation of the syndrome of church development that was described in another chapter. Notice the fallacy: the decision as to the future direction of the mission is taken on the basis of the *church* that is already there rather than on the basis of the *challenge* to win thousands of people in the community who do not yet know Jesus personally. Missonaries should not consider themselves out of a job until every conceivable winnable person is won to Christ and continuing faithfully in the apostles' doctrine, in fellowship, in breaking of bread, and in prayers.

360-degree missions—missions go full circle when the new church that is planted by the first mission gives birth to a mission of its own. The old indigenous church principle of a self-propagating church too often referred only to the 270-degree position—a church that would be capable of keeping itself alive. But the 360-degree position insists that this church not only keep itself going, but also generate other churches in other cultures. In other words, a 360-degree church is a missionary-minded church.

Generally speaking, our missionary work over the past 150 years has been 270-degree work. We have planted many indigenous *churches* and denominations, but we have not adequately stressed planting indigenous *missions*. Chua Wee Hian, general secretary of the International Fellowship of Evangelical Students, wrote back in 1969, "Most of my missionary friends confess that they have never preached a single sermon on missions to the young churches." I think he is right. While on furlough, missionaries preach wonderful sermons to fire up their friends for missions. But when they get back to the field they do not preach those sermons. Missionaries themselves unconsciously propagate the idea that missions is a Western task. The feet are all white!

A Decade of Research

In 1971 a major consultation of IFMA and EFMA mission executives was called in order to discuss relationships between missions and national churches. Four-hundred top leaders met in Green Lake, Wisconsin for a week, wrestling with the problems that faced them all. Although it had some minor shortcomings, it was an excellent conference in itself. Evangelicals have seen nothing like it before or since. However, at Green Lake it was still assumed that missions were Western missions. The missionaries' feet were still white.

Nevertheless, Green Lake was a milestone because there a new research trend began. The change did not come in the program itself; it came through conversation in the corridors as participants began to realize that there was a gap between 270-degree missions and 360-degree missions. A major catalyst was a Korean team, David Cho and Samuel Kim, an executive and a missionary of a third-world mission, Korea International Mission. They should have had a prominent part on the program, but they didn't because the conference planning had been bogged down at the 270-degree quadrant.

I do not mean to imply that the executives at Green Lake were ignorant of what was occurring in other parts of the world, such as Korea. Most were aware that some third-world churches were sending missionaries out. A fine address on the subject had been delivered to EFMA executives as early as 1962 by Louis L. King of the Christian and Missionary Alliance. But at Green Lake the matter simply was not yet considered that *important* for a North American missionary consultation.

The steering committee at Green Lake commissioned two books. One was a compendium of the papers and proceedings, edited by Vergil Gerber, with the title *Missions in Creative Tension.* To supplement that, they asked me if

I would undertake editing a new symposium which represented the thinking of key participants after they had received the input of Green Lake. The volume, now out of print, was entitled *Church/Mission Tensions Today.* I invited thirteen leaders to participate, and especially asked three of them to contribute chapters on third-world missions. Grady Mangham of the Christian and Missionary Alliance wrote a chapter on the outstanding progress that his mission had made in helping Asian churches to go 360 degrees. Ian Hay of SIM International described how the West African churches had already established a mission board and sent out 100 missionary couples. And Ralph Winter, now of the U.S. Center for World Mission, dealt with the missiological aspects in a brilliant chapter called "Planting Younger Missions."

Once this happened, it seemed that interest in 360-degree missions perked up all over the place. More information was needed. Exactly what was happening out there in the third world? In order to answer this question, a small research team was organized at the Fuller School of World Mission. The team was composed of James Wong, Edward Pentecost, and Peter Larson. I had the privilege of coaching them. Several months of intensive research by the team led to the publication of their book in 1973, *Missions from the Third World*—the first global account of third-world missions.

Later on, Professor Marlin L. Nelson of the Asian Center for Theological Studies and Mission in Seoul, Korea, did his doctoral work at Fuller on third-world missions. Two books resulted in 1976. The first was a fine in-depth study of Asian missions entitled *The How and Why of Third World Missions*. The second was a key document which will bolster any future research in the field called *Readings in Third World Missions*. It includes a laboriously compiled, annotated bibliography of over 300 docu ments relating to the subject, plus reprints of the thirty most significant contributions.

The latest chapter in the research saga, at this writing, came out of another Fuller doctoral program done in 1981 by Lawrence E. Keyes, now president of Overseas Crusades. Building on all the previous research, and launching an extensive survey of his own, Keyes' book with the title *The Last Age of Missions* has been a tremendous encouragement to the Christian world in general. It is a fitting climax to the process begun ten years earlier in Green Lake.

Before sharing the specifics of this decade of research, some terms need to be defined.

Defining the Third World

In the first chapter, I briefly discussed the term *third world* as referring generally to Asia, Africa, and Latin America. It might be helpful at this stage to refine the definition somewhat. We need to know what part of the world we are including and what part we are excluding. Some countries are easy to place. For example, the United States, Russia, and Germany are clearly not third world. Burundi, Cambodia, and Bangladesh clearly are. What is the criterion?

It cannot be strictly *economic*. We cannot say that only the underdeveloped countries are third world. That would exclude countries such as Japan or Korea.

It cannot be strictly *political*. If you say that third-world nations are those nonaligned to the Communist or to the capitalist worlds, you would leave out China or Ethiopia.

It cannot be strictly *geographical*. There are third-world peoples on all continents. As a matter of fact, right here in the U.S.A. we have third-world peoples, such as many of our blacks, Hispanics, Indians, and Orientals.

As I see it, the definition of third world is best considered as *social-psychological.* The group mentality of a people places them in the third world. This mentality means that a certain people feel themselves independent to some significant degree of the two great Western power blocs, although of course hardly anyone in today's shrinking world can claim absolute independence. Granted, this *social-psychological* definition is not cut-and-dried enough to be reduced to some mathematical formula, but experience has shown that it is as useful as any other. By it South African blacks, East Indians, mainland Chinese, Colombians, and many others like them feel that they have certain important things in common. A high-level conference for third-world theologians was held in Seoul, Korea in 1982, for instance, and this by and large was the criterion used to determine who qualified.

Defining Missions

We know that one thing happening among third-world peoples is that they are beginning to send out missionaries to propagate the Christian faith. What do we mean by *missionaries* in this context? Throughout this book we have been stressing that missionaries are those sent to spread the gospel across cultural boundaries. This is still the basic definition, but there is one category of missionary that it would not include—those missionaries, for example, who are sent by the Japanese church to plant churches among Japanese colonists in Brazil. They go a long way geographically, but do not cross cultures.

Some technical terminology is helpful at this point. Missiologists find it useful to distinguish between E-1, E-2, and E-3 missions. The *E* stands for evangelism and the number stands for the cultural distance you need to go to accomplish it.

E-1 (evangelism-one) describes sharing Christ with those of your own culture, or monocultural evangelism.

Notice that geography is not a significant factor here. E-1 missionaries can travel halfway around the world to do their work. Take, for example, the twenty-two Korean missionaries sent to West Germany by the Full Gospel Central Church of Seoul, Korea. All of them are E-1 missionaries because they are working with first-generation Koreans in West Germany. In fact 56 percent of the 323 missionaries now sent from all of Korea are E-1 workers.

E-2 and E-3 (evangelism-two and evangelism-three) describe sharing Christ with those of a different culture, or cross-cultural evangelism. The distinction between the two is simply that E-3 indicates a culture which is a great deal different from the missionary's own culture, while E-2 is a different culture, but somewhat similar. Again, geography need play no part in this distinction, although it often does. One of the Korean missions, for example, is called Korea Harbor Evangelism. Some of their missionaries are sent to port cities right in Korea to minister to the seamen who come and go. These missionaries are doing both E-2 and E-3 work in their own country. If they evangelize Japanese or Singaporean or Taiwanese seamen it is probably an E-2 experience, while work with French or Nigerian or Libyan seamen would be more E-3 for them.

While in this terminology the *E* stands for evangelism, it also needs to be understood that not all missionaries go specifically to evangelize. Some go for the purpose of *nurturing* the believers through Bible teaching, pastoral care, church development, and other ministries. Others go for *service* such as social ministries, flying airplanes, linguistic work, teaching missionaries' children, operating printing presses and other such ministries. So in the literature sometimes the *E* will be used in a general way to cover all kinds of ministry, while in more technical work *N* (nurture) and *S* (service) will also be introduced.

The most complete missionary directory I know of

from any nation is the *Directory of Korean Missionaries and Mission Societies 1982* edited by Marlin L. Nelson. Not only does it list the names and addresses of the forty-seven Korean sending agencies, but it does the same for each of the 323 Korean missionaries. Then under each missionary Nelson has a symbol which gives the above information. For example, Rev. and Mrs. Lee Eun-Moo, missionaries to Indonesia under the Korea International Mission, are FM-3-E or foreign missionaries at an E-3 culture distance and doing primarily evangelism. Then again, Rev. and Mrs. Lee Joon-Kyo, missionaries to Egypt under the Presbyterian Church of Korea, are classified as FM-1-N which means that, while they are foreign missionaries (*FM*), their work is primarily nurturing (*N*) Korean Christians (*E-1*) who live in Cairo. The missionaries working among seamen in Korean ports are classified as *HM* rather than *FM* because they are home missionaries in this sense.

The kind of work that Nelson has done on this directory is tedious, but if it were multiplied in nations across the world it would be an incalculable help toward advancing the cause of world evangelization.

What the Statistics Show

The international survey done by Wong, Pentecost, and Larson in 1972 identified 3,404 workers serving under 203 third-world sending agencies. Larry Keyes's 1980 update listed 368 agencies sending over thirteen thousand missionaries in 1980, conservatively projected to over fifteen thousand by the end of 1981. If that rate of increase continues, the third-world Protestant missionary force may project to over fifty thousand by the end of the century.

By continents the comparison looks like this:

| | Number of agencies | | % of total |
	1972	1980	1980
Asia	108	208	56%
Africa	27	104	28%
Latin America	61	56	15%
Western	7		1%
	203	368	100%

While Asia leads in the number of agencies, Africa leads in the total number of missionaries with approximately fifty-nine hundred compared to five thousand for Asia. It should also be noted that the rate of growth is highest in Africa. In Latin America the number of agencies declined, but the total number of missionaries increased from 820 to 952 over the eight years. Nigeria and India are sending over two thousand missionaries each, while Ghana and Kenya are sending over one thousand each. Other leading countries with over 500 include Burma (988), Brazil (693), South Africa (579), and the Philippines (544).

New Names in Mission History

All this is not so new as most people think. A few of our well-known Western missions have been working on this for some time, but they are all too few. The Christian and Missionary Alliance, the SIM International, the Southern Baptists, and the Overseas Missionary Fellowship are four that have made substantial contributions. Others have much to learn from them. But third-world missions go back farther than that.

In the 1820s, for example, missionaries like Josua Mateinaniu were hopping from one island to another in the Pacific. This is one reason why Oceania is almost entirely

Christian today. In 1827 the Anglican Church Missionary Society, stunned by the extremely high death rate among Europeans in Africa, set up the Fourah Bay Institute in Sierra Leone for training African missionaries. In the 1830s, some Jamaicans, led by Joseph Merrick, pioneered the missionary movement to the Cameroons. By 1884, Methodist missionaries were going out from India to Malaysia. In 1907, the Korean Presbyterians began sending missionaries, among the first being Lee Kee-Pung. One of history's most effective missionary societies, called the Melanesian Brotherhood, was organized in the 1920s in Oceania. Having taken vows of poverty, celibacy, and obedience, Ini Kopuria and other great heroes of the faith went out, barefoot and bareheaded, to propagate the gospel.

Names like Hudson Taylor and Adoniram Judson and Robert Moffat are well-known in missionary history. But Josua Mateinaniu, Joseph Merrick, Lee Kee-Pung, and Ini Kopuria are taking their place with them as the real, worldwide history of missions is being written. Most of the protagonists of our missionary biographies still have white feet, but the color is rapidly changing.

Missions at Bargain Prices

Third-world missions are able to do some things that seem unreal to traditional Western missions. You will remember, for example, that in a previous chapter I mentioned that it costs about $30,000 per year to maintain a U.S. missionary family on the field. Well, the Evangelical Missionary Society (EMS) of Nigeria, an agency related to the Evangelical Churches of West Africa, is sending out 230 missionary couples on a total yearly budget of $250,000 dollars for the whole mission! This figures to just about $1,000 per couple. If, as I contend, good missionary strategy needs to be efficient, there is some efficiency factor built in here that others of us can learn from. A thirty-to-one ratio is highly significant to say the least.

How do they do it?

One clue comes from a series of mimeographed reports I received from survey teams led by the EMS secretary, Panya Baba. The reports describe new areas, attempt to locate the most responsive peoples, make recommendations for church planting, suggest the number of missionaries needed, and then a section follows: "How the Evangelist Might Make a Living." This report assumes that the missionaries will so identify with the people, that they will make their own living right where they minister. Among the possible occupations are poultry raising, vegetable gardening, growing fruit trees, tailoring, and merchandising. Tentmaking is part of the life-style of many third-world missionaries.

Cultural adaptation is another factor. While many Western missionaries are living on subsistence incomes when compared to their own country's standard of living, that same income is often far above the subsistence level in their adopted culture. But third-world missionaries, also willing to live on subsistence income, find that the actual amount is much less than their Western counterparts. In Nigeria the EMS salary, for example, is only one-third the government salary level for unskilled workers, yet Panya Baba says that he receives no complaints from his workers.

The Christian Nationals Evangelism Commission raises funds in the U.S. to support national workers abroad. By nature, they must deal with the salary problem constantly. They report that, in the context of the local economy, an equitable allowance for a rural church planter in Bangladesh is $720 per year, for an urban evangelist in Argentina $10,200 per year, for a village evangelist in

India $720 per year, and for a church planter in Korea $2,500 per year.

Is this unfair? The field workers from the third-world missions do not think so. Many are so excited by the way God is using them that income is strictly a secondary consideration. For example, the state of Rajasthan in Northern India was commonly known as the "wilderness of the gospel." British and American missionaries had worked there for hundreds of years with no real indigenous church movement resulting. But then a third-world mission called Gospel for Asia moved in with Indian missionaries from South India, clearly an E-2 task for them. One of their workers, K. P. Yohannon says in a 1982 *Christian Life* interview: "This year, in just three months, we have seen new churches planted in over 21 villages. In Jaipur, a major provincial capital, over 1,000 came to Christ in one week alone." Yohannan confirms that these Indian missionaries can operate on around $700 per year average, and then comments: "Of course, this is the same level of poverty at which most nationals live, but the evangelists must live at the same level of the people anyway to lead a mass movement."

In 1958, a group of concerned Indian Christians from the Church of South India held a prayer meeting at Kovilpatty. At that time they formed the Friends Missionary Prayer Band. They worked with local E-1 evangelism for some time, but in 1971 God gave them a vision for North India, an E-2/E-3 challenge. They selected eleven states of North India and asked God to send at least two missionaries to each district of those states in ten years. It added up to 220 districts, so they were praying for 440 missionaries.

They reasoned that each prayer group they organized could support one missionary. The membership requirements for each prayer group include promising funds for missionary support, which makes sense in the light of Jesus' statement that where your treasure is there your heart shall be also. All they would need, they calculated, were 440 prayer groups to reach their goal!

By 1975 the Friends Missionary Prayer Band had sent out fifty-five workers, and by 1981 there were 220 on the field. They have not yet reached their 440, but they are well on the way and growing extremely rapidly, supported by an economy which has a per capita gross national product of $240 per year compared to $11,360 in the U.S.

Let me hasten to say that all this does not mean that we Americans should support our own American missionaries any less, whatever the cost may be. Material considerations must be kept secondary to spiritual considerations. The Great Commission is still mandatory for American churches. A great amount of the blessing of God will leave American churches if they pull back on their personal involvement in recruiting and sending their own people to the unreached of the world. We need more, not fewer, missionaries with white feet. But we all can rejoice that they are no longer alone. Every new black, brown, red, and yellow foot that enters the great company of harvesters sent out to the harvest fields of the world will help hasten that glorious day when those from every tongue, tribe, and nation will proclaim Jesus as their Lord.

Do Something Now!

1. Write to Dr. Lawrence E. Keyes, Overseas Crusades, Box 66, Santa Clara, California 95052, and ask him for a sample copy of his newsletter on third-world missions called "Bridging Peoples." If you find it helpful, you may want to subscribe.

2. Read two books:

The Last Age of Missions: A Survey of Third World Missions by Lawrence E. Keyes (William Carey Library).

As I explained in the text, this is the latest document sharing research on third-world missions.

Readings in Third World Missions: A Collection of Essential Documents edited by Marlin L. Nelson (William Carey Library). This is an annotated bibliography of all writings pertinent to third-world missions up to the mid-seventies with reprints of thirty carefully selected essays.

3. Read *Mission: A World-Family Affair* by Allen Finley and Lorry Lutz (Christian Nationals Press, 1470 N. 4th Street, San Jose, California 95112). Organize a group discussion on the pros and cons of using American funds to support national workers in other countries.

Ten

Becoming a World Christian

One day Jesus taught His disciples a lesson about missions they never forgot. Those disciples were fishermen, so He taught them something about fishing. It's all recorded in Luke 5:4-10.

Jesus related His teaching to the fishermen's own goal: a great catch of fish (v.4). This goal made sense to the disciples because they were *professionals*. All fishermen aren't pros, of course. Some people go fishing just for the enjoyment of being out in the fresh air and getting away from the normal routine of life for a while. Many amateur fishermen get satisfaction from fishing whether they catch anything or not. They *prefer* to catch something, they even make up fantasies when they don't, but they nevertheless go back again and again when they don't. They enjoy the fishing as much as the fish.

Not professionals! They have to take fishing more seriously than that because their livelihood depends on it.

Jesus was talking to *professional* fishermen, but He made it clear that He was not really talking about fish. He said, "From now on you will catch *men*" (v. 10, italics added). This reinforces the Strategy I goal of the Great Commission—to make disciples. Jesus wanted His disciples to take His work at least as seriously as they took their fishing. He wants a great multitude of disciples, and He is not satisfied with less.

There is much amateur thinking in missions today. Amateur thinking is satisfied with fishing without catching. I have heard Christian leaders express ideas which would sound something like this to a fisherman:

• God wants us to fish strenuously for people. He is pleased if we put in long hours, use creative fishing techniques, keep our equipment up-to-date, and read the latest angling literature, but He is not particularly concerned whether we catch anything or not.

• God does not expect us to keep records of how many fish we catch. As long as we keep working hard, He will take responsibility for the results and for keeping track of how well we are doing. We will only know if we have caught anything when we get to heaven.

• A smaller catch of fish is usually a higher *quality* than a large catch, and furthermore they're much easier to keep in the boat. We prefer quality to quantity.

The professional fishermen in Luke's story knew better than that, but nevertheless they had fished all night and caught nothing. They were tired and discouraged. Their program had failed. Like many missionaries today, they had the resources, they had the experience, and they worked hard. But they had been fishing without catching.

Then Jesus came along and said, "Launch out into the deep" (v. 4). I can imagine how this advice from a *carpenter* struck these exhausted *fishermen* when they first heard it. They were disappointed with their evening's performance, but they were tired, they wanted something to eat, and they wanted to get some sleep. Their nets were already washed, and they were reconciled to defeat.

But although Jesus was no fisherman, He was *Lord.* So they argued a little, but they changed their plans and obeyed Him. What they didn't know at the time was that Jesus, with divine wisdom, was applying Strategy II— sending them to the right place at the right time. All night long they had been in the wrong place at the wrong time.

As always, it paid to obey Jesus. They got such a great catch of fish that they filled one of their boats and had to call for the other. If a third boat had been available, that one probably would have been filled as well. The new program was producing results, and the fishermen were delighted.

So was Jesus. His disciples had learned a valuable lesson. They trusted the Lord, and He was able to put them in the right place at the right time.

That phrase *"launch out into the deep"* rings down to us today. It is another of the great missionary commands of the Bible.

Thousands of Christians in North America would like to be more deeply involved in missions. They want to "launch out into the deep" but they don't quite know how. They feel that Jesus has something more for them to do in missions, and they would like to discover what it is. They want to know the right place and the right time.

This whole book has been written precisely to help you find God's specific time and place for you. If you have read the book, you have taken a significant first step. Now here are some concrete hints as to what to do next.

At the end of each of the other chapters there is a section headed, "Do Something Now!" The rest of this final chapter will pick up many of those items and add some others so that those who feel challenged to become world Christians and take some action will know how to start.

How to Pray for Missions

Let's take it from the top. Suppose God is speaking to you and pushing you toward becoming a world Christian. The thing you can do right now is to begin to pray sincerely about it.

My first suggestion is that you find a wall and tack up two items:

1. A contemporary world map (check to see that the Congo is now Zaire and that Ceylon is Sri Lanka for starters).

2. The chart "Unreached Peoples of the World—1983." You can get the paper "refrigerator door" size (12½" by 16½") for two for $1.00 or the larger size (19" by 25") on untearable Kimdura material for only $1.50 postpaid. Order yours from the U.S. Center for World Mission, 1605 Elizabeth Street, Pasadena, California 91104.

Spend some time in front of these posters, asking God to open the eyes of your understanding.

My second suggestion is that you pray individually in your quiet time. There are three items you will find useful to keep you both disciplined and informed in this:

1. *The Frontier Fellowship Prayer Guide,* available also from the U.S. Center for World Mission where you order the chart mentioned above. For $1.00 they will send you both a small chart and a *Prayer Guide* .

2. *Operation World: A Handbook for World Intercession* by Patrick Johnstone. If you can't get it in your local Christian bookstore, write STL Books, Box 28, Waynesboro, Georgia 30830.

3. *Unreached Peoples Prayer Brochures* published by

MARC, 919 W. Huntington Drive, Monrovia, CA 91016. Ask them for samples and a price list.

My third suggestion is that you form a Frontier Fellowship prayer group which meets regularly once a month. For complete instructions as to how to do this, write Frontier Fellowship, 1605 Elizabeth Street, Pasadena, CA 91104.

How to Go to the Mission Field

Part of being a world Christian is getting to the mission field. The length of time you stay depends on a great many factors, but in this day and age if you pray about it and set your goal on traveling to some part of the third world, you probably will make it. There are four levels of involvement you will want to consider:

First, you can go as a career missionary. If you feel that God may be calling you to make a career investment in missions, the first thing to do is to talk to your pastor. He or she may direct you to denominational or interdenominational agencies or both. If you have strong denominational ties in one of the more exclusive denominations such as Southern Baptists or Assemblies of God or Seventh Day Adventists or the like, the most reasonable option is usually your own denomination's mission agency.

But if for any reason you wish to look at a broader range of options, you should take the time to get to know as many mission agencies as well as you can.

When a career is on the line, $20 or $30 is not a huge expenditure. Order your own copy of MARC's *Mission Handbook: North American Protestant Ministries Overseas* (919 W. Huntington Drive, Monrovia, California 91016). This lists 714 agencies and gives the basic information needed for an introduction to each of them. Read it and mark it up. Then write directly to the mission agencies that interest you most and ask them for more information.

When you write, also ask MARC for their attractive, illustrated workbook *You Can So Get There from Here.* It expands a great deal on what I am saying very briefly— how to get to the mission field.

If at all possible, try to attend a large missionary conference where several mission boards will send representatives. America's largest is the Inter-Varsity Missions conference held every three years on the campus of the University of Illinois at Urbana during the Christmas holidays. Almost every American mission agency sets up a booth at Urbana and brings its best people and its best literature. If anything, you need to be careful of information overkill there. For details write to Inter-Varsity Missions, 233 Langdon Street, Madison, Wisconsin 53703.

Other such conferences are held at some large local churches, Bible colleges and seminaries, and in the meetings of some regional missionary associations which have been organized in certain parts of the country. The national meetings of the Association of Church Missions Committees (Box ACMC, Wheaton, Illinois 60187) are also planned to give you a good overview of the various agencies.

My final suggestion is to get in touch with the Intercristo Center for Christian Work Opportunities, Box 33487, Seattle, Washington 98133. Write them in some detail and they will outline the next steps for you to take. They have a computer data bank which lists a large number of current job openings on the mission fields and they can give you information on likely options which match your skills. If you need some direct personal counseling, an Intercristo subsidiary, The Career Directory Co., is available to assist you to establish a realistic career goal and get placed in that position. It is a non-profit organization, but charges modest fees for its services.

Second, you can go as a short-term worker. If you're not

sure about God's call to a career in missions, but have some skill that might be needed, consider short-term service. Short-term workers are usually those in a period of life either before they have children or after their children have left home. Single people, younger couples, and older men and women can all find opportunities for meaningful short-term missionary service.

Again, if you belong to a denominational church, the first place to check is your own denomination's mission agency. Before you do you need a fairly good idea as to how long you can stay. Contracts of one or two years are common.

Intercristo, mentioned above, is often very helpful in placing short-term workers. So is Christian Service Corps, 1509 Sixteenth Street, N.W., Washington, D.C. 20036. If you want information on how you might go as a "tentmaker," write Overseas Counseling Service, 1605 Elizabeth Street, Pasadena, California 91104.

Third, you can go as a summer student. Many excellent opportunities for getting to the mission field are provided for young people still in school or just finished with it. Denominations which have strong programs include Southern Baptists, Assemblies of God, Christian and Missionary Alliance, Conservative Baptists, and many others. Some local churches or youth groups have organized their own summer programs.

The largest interdenominational program is Youth with a Mission, Box 4600, Tyler, Texas 75712. A close second is Teen Missions International, Box 1056, Merritt Island, Florida 32952. If you are interested in Mexico, the Spearhead program sponsored by the Latin America Mission may be for you. Write Box 141368, Coral Gables, Florida 33114. If you want to go to Japan, write Language Institute for Evangelism, P.O. Box 200, San Dimas, California 91773. Your English language will provide you an immediate ministry there. One of the nation's fastest growing summer programs is Inter-Varsity's Student Training in Missions (STIM) with over 200 going out in the summer of 1983. Contact them at 233 Langdon Street, Madison, Wisconsin 53703.

How to Learn More About Missions

An excellent way to learn more about missions is to enroll in a school that specializes in the field. As I have mentioned previously, the number of schools recruiting large faculties in missiology is increasing. At the moment, the ones which have excelled are Asbury Theological Seminary in Wilmore, Kentucky; Biola University in La Mirada, California; Columbia Bible College in Columbia, South Carolina; Dallas Theological Seminary in Dallas, Texas; the Fuller Seminary School of World Mission in Pasadena, California; Mid-America Baptist Theological Seminary in Memphis, Tennessee; Southwestern Baptist Theological Seminary in Fort Worth, Texas; and Trinity Evangelical Divinity School in Deerfield, Illinois.

Some academic institutions have put together special training programs for the summer months. Wheaton College holds a Summer Institute of Missions as does the Fuller School of World Mission. One of the many features of the latter is a special four-week module called the Fuller Institute of Language and Culture Learning, staffed by Tom and Betty Sue Brewster, authors of *Language Acquisition Made Practical* (LAMP), and anthropologist Paul Hiebert. Several mission agencies are using this as a part of their pre-field candidate orientation program. For information write to Dr. Dean S. Gilliland, 135 N. Oakland Avenue, Pasadena, California 91101.

A unique study program designed especially for college students is the Institute for International Studies (1605 Elizabeth Street, Pasadena, California 91104). The IIS holds semester-length courses which can be accredited and transferred into many university programs. Write them if you are a student and would like to spend one of your semesters becoming a world Christian.

Another outstanding pre-field training program is conducted by Agape International, the foreign mission arm of Campus Crusade for Christ. Their thirteen-week program provides intensive training for their own missionary candidates, but other mission agencies use them as well. A feature of their training routine is living for three months in black ghettos of South-Central Los Angeles on the invitation of several of the black churches in the area. For more information write Agape International, Arrowhead Springs, San Bernardino, California 92414.

If it isn't possible for you to get to one of these mission training programs, you can take self-study courses at home. Two of them are particularly recommended:

1. Study missiology with the master. Donald A. McGavran is widely regarded as the twentieth century's most outstanding missiologist. His *magnum opus* is the textbook, *Understanding Church Growth*. I have recorded my own comments on that book and other aspects of missions on six cassette tapes and developed a seventy-four-page workbook which coordinates the textbook with the tapes and provides a twenty-five- to thirty-hour learning experience. It is distributed in an attractive binder under the title *Your Church and Church Growth* by the Charles E. Fuller Institute of Evangelism and Church Growth, Box 989, Pasadena, California 91102.

2. *Perspectives on the World Christian Movement* is a study course based on the 864-page reader by that same name compiled by Ralph D. Winter and Steven C. Hawthorne. It is accompanied by a 170-page study guide called *Understanding the World Christian Movement,* and college credit can be arranged if desired. Write Career

Foundations, 1605 Elizabeth Street, Pasadena, California 91104.

One other high-level training opportunity has some restrictions for those who may consider it. It is called the In-Service Program (ISP) and is sponsored by the Fuller Seminary School of World Mission and directed by Alvin Martin. Courses are for graduate school credit, so it is designed for those who have college degrees. Each course contains about sixteen cassette tapes recorded live in the classroom, plus textbooks, syllabus, assignments, and exams. Five courses taught by Paul E. Pierson, Arthur F. Glasser, Charles H. Kraft, Paul G. Hiebert, and C. Peter Wagner are available. To qualify you must be a college graduate and in ministry (missionaries or nationals) outside of the United States and Canada, or if you live in North America you must be a missionary under appointment, a missionary on furlough, or training others for cross-cultural ministry. For details write In-Service Program, Fuller School of World Mission, 135 N. Oakland Avenue, Pasadena, California 91101.

Another obvious way of learning more about missions is reading books and magazines. I have listed most of the key current books at the end of the chapters, so will not repeat them here. The one that bears repetition is *In the Gap* by David Bryant (Inter-Varsity Missions). If you missed this one before, pick it up now. It is an excellent sequel to this book.

The best way to keep up on the newest literature coming off the presses is to become a member of the Global Church Growth Book Club. This membership is packaged with a subscription to Global Church Growth magazine which announces new selections in every issue. Then you order (at a discount) the books you wish. Send $6.00 for one year to *Global Church Growth,* Box 66, Santa Clara, California 95052.

Only one popular-level Christian magazine is totally devoted to missions. Called *World Christian* (formerly *Today's Mission*) it was founded on a shoestring by a group of graduates from Westmont College, and is expanding rapidly. You can subscribe by sending $12.00 to World Christian Associates, Box 40345, Pasadena, California 91104. World Christian Associates also have many other resources which will help both you as an individual and your church or student group in expanding your horizons.

On a more technical level, *Global Church Growth* which was just mentioned, is an excellent magazine to help you keep up on what is happening in the world. *Evangelical Missions Quarterly* is also must reading for world Christians. It costs $10.00 per year and is available from Evangelical Missions Information Service (EMIS), Box 794, Wheaton, Illinois 60189. EMIS also publishes several other items such as *Missionary News Service* and *Pulse* newsletters from several parts of the world. Ask for a price list when you write. Last but not least, the U.S. Center for World Mission publishes a monthly newspaper called *Mission Frontiers,* available by writing to the U.S. Center at 1605 East Elizabeth Street, Pasadena, California 91104. Subscriptions are $3.00 per year.

To supplement this, keep in mind that each mission agency publishes its own house organ. Simply by making a financial contribution to the agency, you will be placed on their mailing list and receive their magazine. Much of the information I myself get about what is currently happening in missions comes from these periodicals.

Looking Ahead

A good deal of this book has been looking at the past and present to see what God has been and is doing in the world. Let's end by looking forward, looking forward to a very special day. It is described in Revelation 19:7-9: "Let us be glad and rejoice and give Him glory, for the marriage of the Lamb has come, and His wife has made herself ready . . . Blessed are those who are called to the marriage supper of the Lamb!"

Many, when they read this, do not realize that it is a missionary passage. But it is. Notice who the bride is. She is described in Revelation 21:9-10: " 'Come, I will show you the bride, the Lamb's wife.' . . . and the great city, the holy Jerusalem, descending out of heaven from God." For several verses the physical characteristics of the New Jerusalem are described, and then the inhabitants: "The nations of those who are saved shall walk by its light" (Rev. 21:24) and "they shall bring the glory and the honor of the nation into it" (Rev. 21:26). These are the people whose names are written in the Lamb's Book of Life (Rev. 21:27).

Where does this life come from? How does a person receive the life which allows his or her name to be recorded in the Lamb's book? There is one source and one source only—Jesus Christ. "He who has the Son has this life; he who does not have the Son of God does not have life" (1 John 5:12).

So the missionary mandate comes down to allowing God to use us as instruments for sharing His love and life with the peoples of the world. It is the process of preparing the bride of Christ for that glorious day in the future when the wedding takes place. The Great Commission, which I have mentioned so frequently in this book, instructs us to "make disciples of all the nations" (Matt. 28:18-20). The Greek word for nations, *ethne,* is the same word used in Revelation 21 describing the inhabitants of the New Jerusalem, the bride of Christ, as well as in the list of those around the throne of the Lamb who come from "every tribe and tongue and people and nation" singing a new song to the Lord (Rev. 5:9).

How long will this take? No one really knows. Jesus will come like a thief in the night, probably when we least expect Him. But He has told us why He is waiting. In 2 Peter 3 we read in some detail about the end of this present age, and the question comes up as to why God is waiting so long. I like the way *The Living Bible* phrases the answer: "He is giving us time to get his message of salvation out to others" (2 Pet. 3:15).

In my mind there is no question of God's will for these closing years of the twentieth century. We have limited time and 16,750 people groups yet to reach with the gospel. The bride of Christ is not yet ready for the wedding. The most significant and exciting challenge that I know of is to become a vital part of the evangelization of the world.

"And this gospel of the kingdom will be preached in all the world as a witness to all the nations, and then the end will come" (Matt. 24:14).

Index

Fascinating Reading from Regal Books

☐ **Lords of the Earth,** Don Richardson—The fascinating story of the Yali cannibals who serve hateful gods, and of missionary Stan Dale who dared to enter their domain. — $7.95 5405718

☐ **Peace Child,** Don Richardson—Richardson narrates firsthand the gripping account of how the Peace Child brought true peace at last to the Sawi people of Irian Jaya. — $6.95 5403006

☐ **A Distant Grief,** F. Kefa Sempangi with Barbara R. Thompson—A victorious statement about the persecuted Christians in Uganda and a compelling witness to the Western church. — $4.95 5411807

☐ **Eternity in Their Hearts,** Don Richardson—King Solomon's statement that God has set eternity in the hearts of men is proven through fascinating examples of how God enabled different pagan peoples to understand the meaning of the gospel. — $9.95 5108608

☐ **Trapped!** David Dawson—A young physician shares his experiences of being trapped in the combat zone between loyalist troops and advancing guerillas during Zaire's civil war in 1977. — $3.95 5018002

☐ **With Justice for All,** John Perkins—Introduces new and unconventional concepts that will shake Americans to a new understanding of their responsibilities and help awaken America spiritually and economically. — $10.95 5108802

☐ **On the Crest of the Wave,** C. Peter Wagner—Discover how you can have a global impact as part of the world Christian movement. Peter Wagner gives us the facts in this popular, up-to-date missions classic. — $6.95 5418015

Buy these at your local bookstore or use this handy coupon for ordering:

Regal Books, P.O. Box 3875, Ventura, CA 93006
Please send me the book(s) I have checked above. I am enclosing
$ _____ . (Orders under $20.00, add $1.00 shipping and handling, over $20.00 add 10%. All California orders must include 6% sales tax.) Send check or money order—No cash or C.O.D.

Please charge my
  ☐ Visa   Card # _____
  ☐ MasterCard   Exp. Date _____
Name: _____
Address: _____
City: _____ State/Zip: _____

Please allow 2-4 weeks delivery. U.S. prices shown. Prices subject to change without notice.   88557
